CHINA'S
THREATENED
WILDLIFE

CHINA'S
THREATENED
WILDLIFE

LIZ AND KEITH LAIDLER

BLANDFORD

A BLANDFORD BOOK

First published in the UK 1996 by Blandford
A Cassell Imprint
Cassell plc, Wellington House
125 Strand, London WC2R 0BB

Distributed in the United States by Sterling Publishing Co., Inc.
387 Park Avenue South, New York, NY 10016-8810

Distributed in Australia by Capricorn Link (Australia) Pty Ltd
2/13 Carrington Road, Castle Hill, NSW 2154

A Cataloguing-in-Publication Data entry for this title
is available from the British Library

ISBN 0-7137-2372-6

Typeset by Keystroke, Jacaranda Lodge, Wolverhampton, England
Printed and bound in Spain

Previous page: Giant panda (*Ailurus melanoleuca*) feeding on
winter bamboo, Qionglai Mountains, Sichuan Province.

CONTENTS

CONVERSION TABLE

1 millimetre (mm) = 0.03 inch

1 centimetre (cm) = 0.39 inch

1 metre (m) = 1.09 yards

1 kilometre (km) = 0.62 mile

1 hectare (ha) = 2.47 acres

1 gram (g) = 0.03 ounce

1 kilogram (kg) = 2.20 pounds

1 tonne = 0.98 ton

Temperature conversion

$°C = (°F - 32) \times 5 \div 9$

PREFACE

WHEN WE FIRST STARTED TO RESEARCH CHINA'S ANIMALS AND PLANTS IN 1982 for our television documentaries, we were astonished by the rich variety of China's wildlife and wild places. Many plant and animal species, among them the giant panda, Yangtze dolphin, Chinese alligator and Père David's deer are found nowhere else in the world. Twelve years later, after numerous trips to China, and after seeing many of these creatures in environments as beautiful as any on earth, the wonder is, if anything, stronger than ever but it has been tempered by sobering observation.

China's bio-diversity is under threat. We saw for ourselves why the great Yangtze, Son of the Ocean and sustainer of life, can no longer support the Chinese alligator, Yangtze dolphin or Chinese sturgeon. We walked amongst the giant panda's greatly reduced forest home and were shown the problems that human beings pose. And we talked to peasants, scientists and government officials and sympathized with their predicaments and individual

In many provinces, even the highest, most inaccessible areas have been turned over to agriculture.

viewpoints. We had also witnessed such realities in South America, the Caribbean, Africa and Britain: the global problems of people's needs, people's wants, overdevelopment and overpopulation.

China's economy is developing rapidly. Hamstrung for decades by Mao Zedong's political ideals, China is becoming an economic force to be reckoned with. Seven out of ten products are now made in China. The signs of 'Westernization' and increasing affluence are clearly evident. In 1984 when we first visited Beijing, the streams of cyclists travelling to and from work were a sea of blue and green Mao jackets. Two years later, new fashions of all colours had largely replaced the blue-green conformity. To take over a digital watch for a Chinese friend was, at first, a must but, in a year or two, such presents were redundant – they were readily available and affordable in China. Farmers in particular have become wealthier under new free-market policies and everyone's material aspirations are rising, right down to the humblest peasant. The Chinese have become consumers.

Gearing up to a Western-style economy has increased the pressures on habitats but the Chinese have also become more environmentally aware. Not, perhaps, the ordinary man on the street but certainly the country's scientists and its government. In 1985 when we started to organize China's first international conference on wildlife conservation we suggested, with some temerity, an agenda that took account of political, social and economic issues. Much to our relief, it was embraced wholeheartedly. The Chinese were eager to share their problems with other countries and to exchange ideas. The past decade or so has seen genuine attempts to tackle conservation.

Several books have been written recently about Chinese wildlife. Some have concentrated on one or two species, for example, George Schaller *et al.*'s book *The Giant Pandas of Wolong* (1985) and our own book on the giant panda and red panda. Others, such as *The Natural History of China* by Zhao *et al.* (1990) and *Living Treasures* by Tang (1987) look only briefly at the status and conservation problems of individual species. There was a need for a much more detailed account, especially of species that represented the problems of their habitat. This book was written to fill that gap. We dedicate it to our friends in China who have helped us to observe and film wonders that would have been otherwise impossible to achieve and we also dedicate it to the efforts of all those involved in preserving China's unique natural heritage.

Liz and Keith Laidler

CHINA: A WORLD OF ITS OWN

THE ANCIENT CHINESE BELIEVED THAT THEIR LAND WAS THE MIDDLE OF THE Earth so they called it the Middle Kingdom. The modern word for China, *Zhong-guo*, means 'Central Land' and the Chinese still call themselves *Zhong-guo-ren*, 'People of the Central Land'. It is easy to understand why their ancestors believed they occupied such an important position. China is a world of its own. With the exception of the polar tundra, it contains all the ecosystems found in the northern hemisphere and features as many different climates as there are on this planet. There are lush, tropical rainforests; fertile, alluvial plains; cold, mist-shrouded bamboo forests; stony deserts; lakes and marshlands as vast as oceans, and icy, sub-arctic meadows.

The reasons for these varied environments are two-fold. First of all, China is huge. Straddling 50° of latitude (from the shores of the Pacific Coast to the Pamirs) and 60° of longitude (from the River Amur to the Nansha Archipelago, it is the second largest country after Canada, with an area of 9.6 million km². In early spring, when red-crowned cranes in the northern marshes of the Wuyur River Basin are braving the bitter cold, Indian elephants in southern Yunnan are flapping their ears to cool themselves in the baking heat. So, too, the leopard of Manchuria's Changbai Mountains views the dawn when its counterpart in the Tian Mountains of Xinjiang Uygur Autonomous Region is still asleep in its lair.

There is another reason for China's rich diversity. The land rises and falls through extreme altitudinal levels, from the very flat alluvial plains in the east to the jagged heights of the Himalayas that border them in the south-west. In no other country in the world can you travel for 4000 km across unbroken mountain chains (which make up 43 per cent of the country) and another 2000 km across featureless, flat vistas. Other parts of the country are actually below sea level, e.g. the Turpan Depression in Xinjiang. This very varied topography creates dramatic differences in climate between places on the same latitude; at 30° N., the high peaks of the Himalayas experience perpetual winter while Hongku in the Yangtze River (Chang Jiang) Basin swelters in the 32°C heat of summer.

China's vast territory covers two zoogeographical areas: the Palearctic and the Oriental. The northern part of the country, including the Autonomous Regions of Inner Mongolia (Nei Mongol), Xinjiang and most of Tibet (Xizang), belongs to the Palearctic Realm, while the region south of the Qin Mountains belongs to the Oriental Realm. There is a rich diversity of animals within these two realms and many of them are unique to China. There are more than 1000 species and subspecies of birds, comprising 13 per cent of the world's total; over 400 species of mammals (10 per cent of the world's total); 300 species of reptiles and about 200 species of amphibians. Within the plant kingdom, gymnosperms, angiosperms and ferns represent 28.5 per cent, 10.8 per cent and 22 per cent respectively of the world's total. Total plant species number about 35 000 which matches up very well to the richest floras in the world, such as the Malaysian, which boasts about 40 000 species; that of India and Sri Lanka, which supports some 30 000 species; and the tropical rainforests of Central and South America and of Africa. There is also a high degree of endemism in China's plants – more than half of them are found nowhere else on earth. There is a rich diversity of animals within these two realms and many of them are unique to China.

But China's bio-diversity is under threat. The country's natural heritage is suffering from the global problem of unsustainable exploitation; agricultural expansion, deforestation, pollution, over-hunting, together with the huge and still-expanding human population and its growing aspirations, are causing the degradation of China's natural environment. The social and economic consequences of these activities are revealing themselves with a vengeance. In a recent report by Professor Wang Sung and Dr John MacKinnon for the Chinese Government, the authors chronicle declining fish production and timber yields, scarcity of medicinal plants, and rarity of wildlife, with a number of extinctions, loss of forest and steppes, spreading deserts, worsening soil erosion, lowering of water tables and acid rain. These problems are faced in varying degrees by every country in the world so China in no way stands out from the crowd.

But they have had an effect on China's wild creatures. The populous eastern half of the country has long since seen the demise of most of its wildlife but what is worrying is that even the remote, sparsely populated western half is losing its wild heritage. The huge herds of Mongolian gazelle that Roy Chapman Andrews described in 1932 (cited in Schaller, 1993) are no more. Only small, fragmented populations survive. Those of the Tibetan gazelle, wild yak, Bactrian camel and even blue sheep have been reduced to small pockets as a result of habitat destruction and hunting for the export market in meat and horns. In recent years, this has been made easier with the availability of high-powered rifles and the

Above: Signs of acid rain on mountain peaks in south-west China, far from urban sources of pollution.

Opposite: A small yak herd grazing on upland steppes in north-west Tibet.

building of permanent roads, such as the Karakoram Highway between Pakistan and China. In China, the rare snow leopard has vanished completely in many parts of its range, a victim of decreasing numbers of prey and herdsmen trying to protect their livestock. The Chinese Government currently lists 98 species of mammals, birds and reptiles as endangered and in need of protection. Some species are dangerously close to extinction, such as the Yangtze River dolphin, the wild Chinese alligator, the south China tiger and the crested ibis.

Historically, the relationship between the Chinese people and nature was one of utilization and, wherever possible, control, but with this pragmatism there was always a strong element of admiration and reverence. This respect came largely through the influence of religion. China's religions, from early animism to Daoism and Buddhism, have always had a great deal to say about nature and, without them, the Chinese traditional perception of nature would have been probably quite different. The old animistic religions revered mountains; they were sacred, living entities which were the source of water that nourished the crops below. Climbing them was taboo because it amounted to desecration. Daoism was a nature-centred religion *par excellence* and taught that people should be part of, and flow with, nature rather than dominate it. To a Daoist, nature's services should be engaged for spiritual peace and immortality rather than for material gain. Buddhists set great store by the natural environment. The devout are vegetarian, asserting that animals have a right to

Above: The animals and plants on Mount Emei in Sichuan Province are revered and protected by Buddhist monks living there. These Tibetan macaques never go short of food.

Opposite: Meditating at 'Elegant Sound Pavilion' on Mount Emei, a mountain in Sichuan Province sacred to the Buddhist religion.

life and should not be killed, even for food. In common with Daoists, they see people as part of nature rather than its patriarch but they go even further in believing that animals possess varying levels of consciousness and that enlightenment is possible for them as well for human beings.

This uniquely Chinese mix of nature-respecting religions left its mark everywhere – in painting and sculpture, in calligraphy and in the design of gardens. Chinese gardens mimicked nature and featured miniature mountains, streams and waterfalls. It is telling that, in landscape paintings of the Tang Dynasty, human beings, if present at all, were depicted as tiny figures against overpowering landmarks such as mountains and waterfalls. Kublai Khan, the conquering Mongol emperor who established the Yuan Dynasty, set up China's – and the world's – first nature reserve.

Unfortunately, the influence of the 'nature-centred' ethic was not enough to protect China's environment from the pressures of a burgeoning population. In 1954, just 5 years after the People's Republic of China was founded, the Government's concern for the nation's wildlife resulted in a call for a systematic management policy. This aimed to curb hunting of certain species and to set up nature reserves for the protection of threatened species. But the scheme was difficult to implement in practice and it was subsequently dogged by some of Mao Zedong's more revolutionary campaigns, the first being the Great Leap Forward in 1958. The aim of this campaign was self-sufficiency and one means to this end was to turn agricultural tradition upside-down. Mao's slogan 'grain is the key link' saw wholesale wheat planting as the answer to feeding the population. Fish ponds, which for centuries had provided people with a cheap source of protein, were filled in and planted with wheat. Fields of soybeans and peanuts were replaced by more wheat, as were valuable wildlife habitats, which were dubbed 'desert wildernesses' because they were not 'productive'. At the same time there was a national campaign against the Four Evils: flies, mosquitoes, sparrows and rats. Although understandable in principle, the campaign was misguided in practice as the poisons used to get rid of the grain-robbing sparrows also wiped out whole populations of other birds. The environmentally unfriendly trend continued with the Great Proletarian Revolution, better known as the Cultural Revolution. Scholastic endeavour was deplored and centres of learning and research were closed down. There was great upheaval and it resulted in the very disaster that Mao had wanted to prevent – famine. Shortage of food put huge pressures on China's wildlife resources. Hunting laws were abandoned under a wave of uncontrollable poaching; deforestation accelerated and wilderness areas were rapidly turned into farmers' fields. Ironically, in the same year that the Cultural Revolution was launched (1966), the State Council issued a directive urging all provinces to 'actively protect and reasonably utilize wildlife resources'.

When Deng Xiaoping came on the political scene, China opened up to the outside world. Government bodies and academia forged links with foreign and international institutions in Japan, the USA, Germany and the UK to survey and study various endangered species. One of the first and most highly publicized joint ventures was between the World Wildlife Fund (WWF), now the World Wide Fund for Nature, and China's Ministry of Forestry to study the giant panda in the wild. Another major cooperative project was with the International Crane Foundation to help study and protect rare species of crane. Agreements were signed in 1981 with Japan and Australia to protect the hundreds of bird species that migrate between the two countries and China. The China National Man and Biosphere (MAB) Commission of the United Nations Educational, Scientific and Cultural Organisation (UNESCO) was founded in 1979 and 10 more reserves in China are now attached to the International Network of the MAB programme. China became a signatory to the Convention on International Trade in Endangered Species of Wild Flora and Fauna (CITES). Two bodies execute the provisions of the Convention: the Endangered Species Scientific (ESS) Commission under the Academy of Sciences and the Endangered Species of Wild Fauna and Flora Import and Export Administration under the Ministry of Forestry. The ESS Commission updated lists of endangered animals and started the *China Red Data Book*.

For the first time ever the Chinese were viewing their environmental problems in a global context and this was no more clearly seen that when we participated, as representatives of Cambridge University, in China's first international conference on environmental issues (International Conference on Wildlife Conservation in China, Beijing, 1987). Academic and government bodies happily cooperated in setting an agenda that brought the politics of environmental conservation to bear. We aimed to bring together the interests of economics, industry, sociology and biology with a view to finding realistic solutions.

Since then, the Chinese Government and its scientists have continued to put a great deal of effort into halting the degradation and restoring wilderness areas to sustainable productivity through policy and action. The number of nature reserves has increased dramatically from 383 in 1986 to, at present, 800, totalling over 440 000 km² or 5 per cent of the country. Originally, the aim was for 500 reserves by the end of the century to provide an effective protection network for threatened and vulnerable species. This goal has been achieved and bettered and the present reserves include virtually all biotopes and the major populations of endangered animals. Some reserves are large, e.g. the Taxkorgan Reserve in south-western Tibet, which is 5400 km² in extent, the 17 000-km² Arjin Shan Reserve at the northern edge of the Tibetan Plateau and the largest, the Chang Tang Reserve of northern Tibet, which, at 150 000 km² in area, is larger than the UK. Chinese scientists have also gone a long way towards cataloguing the country's bio-diversity through collections and publications. The Government has passed new laws to protect the environment and is promoting modern policies of land management. The conversion of grasslands to fields has been discouraged and privately owned woodlands are now allowed, giving people an incentive to plant and care for trees. The Chinese Government has also joined many international conventions and programmes, e.g. the World Heritage Programme and the Ramsar Convention, and has been cooperating with organizations worldwide such as WWF, International Union for the Conservation of Nature and Natural Resources (IUCN), MacArthur Foundation and Global Environment Fund (GEF) on bio-diversity conservation. The international element is very important and, in recognition of this, China has created a new body – the Chinese Council for International Cooperation in Environment and

Cool temperate coniferous forest

Temperate mixed coniferous and deciduous broadleaf forests

Warm temperate deciduous broadleaf forest

Subtropical evergreen broadleaf forest

Tropical monsoon rainforest and tropical rainforest

Desert

Lowland steppe

Alpine vegetation

MONGOLIA

XINJIANG

KASHMIR

INNER MONGOLIA (NEI MONGOL)

GANSU

NINGXIA

QINGHAI

TIBET (XIZANG)
QINGHAI-TIBET PLATEAU

NEPAL

BHUTAN

BANGLADESH

INDIA

BURMA

VIETNAM

LAOS

THAILAND

KAMPUCHEA

MALAYSIA

INDONESIA

HEILONGJIANG

JILIAN

LIAONING

NORTH KOREA

SOUTH KOREA

Beijing

TIANJIN

HEBEI

SHANXI

SHANDONG

SHAANXI

Yellow River

HENAN

JIANGSU

ANHUI

Shanghai

HUBEI

ZHEJIANG

Poyang Lake

JIANGXI

Yangtze River

SICHUAN

HUNAN

GUIZHOU

FUJIAN

TAIWAN

YUNNAN

GUANGDONG

GUANGXI

Guangzhou (Canton)

HAINAN

PHILIPPINES

BRUNEI

MALAYSIA

INDONESIA

0 250 500 750 1000 km

1:25 000 000

JAPAN

Development (CCICED). This, report Wang and MacKinnon, is a 'high-level vehicle for expanding international cooperation on environment and development and making specific recommendations to the State Council'. Of great international significance is the fact that China is the most powerful developing nation to sign, and, more importantly, ratify, the 1992 Rio Earth Summit Convention on Biological Diversity. Moreover, China has started to implement the Convention even before it comes into force. The USA did not sign the Convention primarily because of political pressure from companies whose vested interests would be affected by proposals to give developing countries a cut of any profits made from potential products discovered in their forests. The Chinese are taking a wide perspective and recognize the long-term benefits, both economic and cultural, to be gained in operating more sustainably. They ratified the convention as early as January 1993, the first major power to do so. Wang and MacKinnon value the present benefits of China's natural resources at many billion US dollars per annum. This can only increase if wildlife resources improve.

Putting environmental conservation high on the political agenda has not come too soon for China's wildlife. There are major problems to be overcome. Market incentives, serious lack of coordination and clear authority, lack of funds, equipment and experienced manpower and the sheer complexity – social, economic and political – of some problems makes for slow progress. Wang and MacKinnon comment that this, in effect, means that 'Even where excellent regulations exist, standards of ground implementation remain very weak'. Those species listed as threatened or endangered 10 years ago are still on the list and many are actually more endangered now. Given the long time-frame of the conservation task, it is not altogether surprising that things should get worse before they get better.

VEGETATION ZONES

It is not our intention to chronicle all of China's threatened or endangered species comprehensively. We would end up with a bulky tome of several hundred pages which would largely duplicate the *China Red Data Book*. Here, we focus principally on the larger, most endangered animals and birds because they tend to be the ones most hunted or most affected by environmental damage and they are also 'flagship' species which represent various ecosystems. To save them from extinction would be to save whole vegetation zones. There are eight such zones and the species are grouped according to those they inhabit. A more detailed coverage of each is given later in the book.

As references are made to provinces and autonomous regions in the summary of the eight vegetation zones below, it is relevant first to describe the country's political and administrative divisions (see map, opposite). There are 23 provinces and 5 autonomous regions. Each province is divided into counties, each of which has its own administrative arm. Han Chinese comprise 90 per cent of the population, the rest being made up of 55 minority groups, or tribes, with cultures and traditions quite different from those of the Han Chinese.

Broadly speaking the vegetation zones run east to west across China in parallel bands. However, at a regional level, China's varied topography makes for a confusing picture – a

Opposite: The eight major vegetation zones and the provinces of China.

single mountain can support a whole range of vegetation types from tropical forest at its base through deciduous and coniferous woodlands to alpine meadows and perpetual shows.

For convenience, in the main body of the book we have subsumed the three northern forest zones discussed in the introduction (cool temperate coniferous forests; temperate mixed coniferous and deciduous broadleaf forests; and warm temperate deciduous broadleaf forests) under a single heading – 'northern forests and wetlands'. By contrast, on the eastern plains of China the natural vegetation type – subtropical evergreen broadleaf forests – has been almost completely destroyed, and only in the west does a vestige of its former glory remain. Accordingly, we have divided this particular vegetation zone into two separate sections: 'Eastern Plains and Yangtze Wetlands' and 'China's Lost Worlds: Temperate Montane Forests'.

Cool temperate coniferous forests

The vegetation type of this zone is typical Siberian taiga, an expanse of mainly coniferous trees that shed their leaves in the long, cold winter. Only Scots pine, Korean spruce and a few others retain their leaves. These forests grow in the northernmost part of China, mainly in the north-western corner of Heilongjiang Province, and are part of the broad band of taiga that extends across Eurasia at these latitudes. Their southern limits are the low northern mountains of the Da Hinggan Range (average altitude 1000 m). The climate is very cold in this part of the world. Winter lasts 9 months and the average annual temperature is 0°C. Only a quarter of the year is frost free and there is permafrost in some parts. Among the dominant species of conifer are Korean spruce, Mongolian Scots pine and Dahurian larch. The dominant broadleaf species are Dahurian birch, Mongolian oak, David's poplar and Manchurian white birch. These trees all have a very short growing period and complete their annual cycles in just a few months. Dahurian larch is well adapted to the cold and forms about half of the total forest area. The forests are edged with shrubs such as Dahurian rhododendrons, cowberry, grasses and sedges.

Temperate mixed coniferous and deciduous broadleaf forests

This vegetation type covers the three mountain ranges of Manchuria: the Da Hinggan Mountains in the west, the Xiao Hinggan Mountains in the north and the Changbai Mountains in the east. These mountains have an average elevation of 1000 m but some peaks rise up to twice this height. The climate is one of warm summers, produced by the moderating effect of the Pacific Ocean, and cold winters. Winter temperatures usually range between –14 and –25°C but can fall to –40°C. When we visited Changbai one October, the temperature was already below freezing. Summer temperatures rise to 20–24°C and this, together with moderate rainfall (500–1000 mm) sustains dense forest growth. The Xiao Hinggan and Changbai Mountains are known in China as the home of the Korean pine as this is the dominant, most widespread forest species. Growing to a height of 30–40 m and with a lifespan of several hundred years, this stately tree is an important symbol of longevity and has featured in many a Chinese painting through the

Opposite: China's 'lost world': the temperate montane forests of Sichuan.

centuries. Further south, the forest changes from mainly coniferous to a mix of coniferous and broadleaf trees, the main species being Mongolian oak. As the mountains are not particularly high, the forests grow right over the tops. Important plant species are Manchurian ash, several maples, Japanese yew, Amur cork tree and ginseng.

The forested mountains surround what used to be a huge, marshy lowland plain. The marshes constitute a quite different ecosystem within this vegetation zone. Most have been drained for agriculture (the area is now known as the 'Great Northern Granary') but some still remain and are home to many migratory birds.

Warm temperate deciduous broadleaf forests

This region is where China's civilization arose and evolved. It is a huge alluvial plain created mainly from loess deposited by the Huang (Yellow) River and also from the sediments of the Huai and Hai Rivers. It extends from the southern part of Liaoning Province to Shandong Peninsula, the North China Plain and the Loess Plateau. It is hot and wet in summer and dry in winter (annual average temperature is 8–16°C. Spring is a season of dust-laden winds, a time of year when bicyclists don their dust masks. Rainfall averages 800 mm on the coast and half that further to the west. China's early civilization evolved from here; the country's ancient capital city, Xian, is located here as is the modern capital, Beijing. The natural forest cover is deciduous broadleaf forest but this is almost non-existent now because of centuries of agriculture. What forest is left (8 per cent of the zone's area) is mainly secondary, consisting largely of maple, oaks, Japanese red pine and Chinese pine. Some tall (20 m) Chinese pines growing near ancient temples are probably remnants of the original forest cover. Several hundred years old, they now overlook fields of grain and cotton.

Desert

China's deserts are concentrated mainly in the north-west and extend over 1 million km^2, covering an eighth of the country. About 60 per cent is sandy desert and the remainder is stony desert. The hot, dry conditions make it a hostile place to live in. There is less than 200 mm of rain a year, some places receiving only 6 mm. In most parts, the huge daily and annual variations in temperature present an enormous challenge to all life forms and so, not surprisingly, this is the least diverse of the vegetation zones. The almost constant gale-force winds add to the battle of life here as they not only exacerbate the effect of the cold and the heat but also create brutal sandstorms that abrade everything in their path. The desert soils are poor and often salty, and vegetation is minimal or absent in many parts, being limited to short scrubby plants that are adapted to arid conditions.

Lowland steppe

The bulk of China's low steppe lands occur on the inner Mongolian Plateau which runs from the eastern foot of the Qilian Mountains north-east to the Da Hinggan Mountains. It is an ancient plateau, some 1000–1300 m high, which has acquired its characteristic flatness

Opposite: Sparse vegetation and high levels of wind erosion characterize China's stony desert.

through millennia of erosion. Winters are cold and windy and summers are influenced by the Pacific monsoon, even though this is considerably weakened by the time it reaches the plateau. The result is a semi-arid climate with no more than 350 mm of rain a year but enough to produce a steppe-land vegetation. In the east the grasses grow as tall as a man but the vegetation gradually downgrades to desert towards the west.

Alpine vegetation/Qinghai-Tibet Plateau

At over 4000 m above sea level, the Qinghai-Tibet Plateau is the highest on earth and is commonly known as the 'Roof of the World'. It is a flat, open landscape bordered on all sides by mountains, walls of permanent snows and glaciers that are among the highest in the world – the Himalayas to the south, the Karakorams in the west, the Kunlun and Qilian ranges in the north and the Tanggula in the east. It is cold and bleak here and travellers are buffeted by an incessant, howling wind with no chance of any shelter among trees, for none can grow here. Even in midsummer snow flurries are not unusual and the ground

The nomad's yurt provides the only shelter on the cold, bleak Qinghai-Tibet Plateau.

is frozen in the early morning. The soils are generally thin and poor and, with an annual rainfall of only 200 mm, they can support only mountain steppe and alpine meadow vegetation and mountain scrub. The plateau is dotted with numerous inland-draining salt lakes and several basins. Only 0.5 per cent of China's population (5.5 million) live on the plateau although it makes up 23 per cent of the country's total land area (2.2 million km² – 90 times the size of the UK).

Subtropical, evergreen, broadleaf forests/eastern monsoon region

This region covers about a quarter of China, bounded in the north by the Qin and Daie Mountains, in the south by the Xi River, in the west by the Qinghai-Tibet Plateau and in the east by the Pacific coast. The area has a subtropical monsoon climate with mild winters (the temperature usually staying above freezing) and hot summers (July temperatures are 25–30°C. The annual rainfall is about 100–2600 mm, some of it falling in winter, conditions broadleaved evergreens thrive on. However, the intensity of human habitation means that very little of this forest remains in its virgin state. What does remain is confined to the higher mountain slopes where agriculture is not possible. The key mountain ranges are the Qin Mountains in the northern limits of the region, and the Min Mountains in Sichuan. These are havens for an abundance of animals and plants, many of which are endemic. Fruit trees, such as tangerine, lychee, longan and pomelo, occur in the south-eastern hills, and further west, growing in panda habitat, are well-known living fossils such as the dawn redwood (dinosaur) tree, the Katsura, the Cathay silver fir, and also the endemic dove tree, the gingko (maidenhair) tree and numerous species of valuable medicinal plants.

Tropical monsoon rainforest and tropical rainforest

Tropical forests extend across the southernmost 3 per cent of China, beyond the tropic of Cancer, i.e. the southern parts of Yunnan, Guangxi, Guangdong and Fujian Provinces and Taiwan, and all of Hainan Island and the South Sea islands. It is the smallest vegetational zone in China but by far the richest, both in the total number of plant species and in the number of endemics. The hot, rainy climate encourages luxuriant plant growth but, as in the eastern monsoon region, much of the original forest has given way to crops and villages so that only a fraction of natural vegetation remains. The two types of rainforest are very similar in structure and share many plant and animal species. The main difference is that the monsoon rainforest, being further north, experiences a rainy and a dry season whereas, in the tropical rainforest proper, the heavy rainfall is spread out through the year.

NORTHERN
FORESTS
AND
WETLANDS

MANCHURIA IS THE MOST NORTH-EASTERLY OF ALL CHINA'S MANY REGIONS. It comprises four provinces: Heilongjiang to the north, Jilin in the middle, Liaoning in the south and, to the west, part of Inner Mongolia (Nei Mongol Autonomous Region). The Manchurian climate is characterized by short, hot summers and long winters of biting cold. For example, the mean January temperature in Harbin, capital of Heilongjiang Province, is −19°C but, in July, the same figure is 22.8°C. The south-eastern monsoon exerts the least influence here than in any other part of eastern China, arriving in a depleted state around the middle of July and bringing with it the season of maximum rainfall.

Manchuria is a land of mountains, plains and wetlands. To the north the Xiao Hinggan range lies north-west/south-east along the border with the former USSR. The Da Hinggan Mountains in the east run on a north-east/south-west axis, as do the Changbai Mountains, which form the border with North Korea. Together, these ranges describe a huge semi-circle of highland with an average elevation of 1000 m, although many of the peaks rise to twice this height. To the south lie the Jehol range and other smaller mountain systems. Overall, the mountain ranges effectively form the sides of an enormous bowl, enclosing the low-lying central plain, which in places is only 50 m above sea level.

Much of the central plain has been colonized by people and converted to agricultural production (maize, sorghum, wheat, flax and soybeans are the main products of the region).

Previous page: The moss-strewn conifers of Manchuria's northern forests form a continuous blanket with the Siberian taiga.

Above: Despite the intense cold of the Manchurian winter, mayflies and other insects abound in summer in the northern forests.

In the past, when the area was known as the 'Great Northern Uncultivated Land', many wetlands were drained to increase land area for production, but several of the surviving marsh and lake systems have since been included in China's network of nature reserves. At 8640 km², the Sanjiang Plain is China's major wetland area.

The forests, too, have felt the effects of human activity. As a major source of lumber for Chinese industry, they have been logged heavily, and recent natural disasters, in the form of extensive forest fires (which in the late 1980s destroyed millions of hectares of northern woodland) have also depleted reserves. However, so large are these forests that, at present, sufficient remains to support a wealth of wildlife.

Manchuria's mountain forests fall into three distinct types:

1. Cool temperate coniferous forests are found in China only within a small area of Manchuria, in the north-western section of Heilongjiang Province, extending south to 46° 26′ N. along the Da Hinggan Mountains. Winters last 9 months in these forests, with spring, summer and autumn crammed into the remaining quarter of the year. There are frosts on 265–285 days of the year, with permafrost (iced subsoil where, even in summer, the thaw does not reach) in the colder areas. Coniferous species predominate, especially Korean spruce (*Picea koraiensis*) in the wet soils of the valley floor, and Dahurian larch (*Larix gmelinii*), which forms the climax species in many areas and occupies about 50 per cent of the total forest area. In this habitat are found wolverine (*Gulo gulo*), Manchurian tiger (*Panthera tigris altaica*) northern lynx (*Felis lynx lynx*) and Siberian ground squirrel (*Citellus* sp.)

2. Temperate mixed coniferous and deciduous broadleaf forest is the most common of the forest types to be found in Manchuria, comprising most of the tree cover on the Xiao Hinggan Mountains and completely dominating the Changbai range. The trees here do not have to withstand as rigorous a climate as the cool temperate coniferous species. Frost-free days number between 100 and 150 each year.

Being closer to the moderating effects of the Pacific Ocean, the spring to autumn period is significantly longer, with warm summers (temperatures can rise as high as 24°C in July and August). As its name suggests, there is a mix between coniferous and deciduous in this woodland, with Korean pine (*Pinus koraiensis*) dominating the coniferous species. This tree grows to a height of 30–40 m and is wonderfully straight, with red bark and wood and a slight but distinctive odour, qualities that have made it a favourite for the building of temples. Deciduous varieties, such as the rare largeleaf ash (*Fraxinus rhyncophylla*), Mongolian oak (*Quercus mongolica*) and Manchurian ash (*F. mandshurica*) gradually increase in prominence as one moves south. Manchurian ash, together with Amur cork tree (*Phellodendron amurenses*) and Japanese oak are relicts from the Tertiary Period, some 60 million years BP. Animal inhabitants include Manchurian tiger (*Panthera tigris altaica*), elk (*Alces alces*), roe deer (*Capreolus capreolus*), bears (*Orsus* spp.), wild boar (*Sus scrofa*) and racoon dog (*Nyctereutes procyonoides*).

3. Warm temperate deciduous broadleaf forests are found in the mountains of a small area of Liaoning Province in southern Manchuria and are more typical of the forest vegetation on China's eastern plains. The climate here is much more affected by the monsoon,

especially towards the coast, with cold winters (–5 to –17°C in January) and hot, rainy summers (21–25°C in July). Rainfall can be as high as 1200 mm in the eastern mountain area, with 60 per cent of the rain falling between June and August. Japanese red pine (*Pinus densiflora*), Chinese pine (*P. tabulaeformis*) and maple (*Acer* spp.) are the dominant tree species on the lower-lying mountains. Where the altitude rises above 1600 m species common to the more northern forests begin to appear.

Wetlands and lakes in this region form a vital part of the migratory pattern of many bird species and several rare forms use the lakes as their summer feeding and breeding area. The Zhalong Nature Reserve, situated close to the town of Qiqihar in Heilongjiang Province is a typical example of a Manchurian wetland, providing a home for at least six of the nine species of crane found in China, including the rare red-crowned crane (*Grus japonensis*), white spoonbill (*Platalea leucorodia*) and two species of stork (*Ciconia ciconia* and *C. nigra*). Various species of goose (*Anser* spp.), swans (*Cygnus* spp.) and ducks such as mallard (*Anas platyrhynchos*) and mandarin (*Aix galericulata*), can also be found in the area.

The mountains and central plain that comprises Manchuria has proved to be a zoological 'mixing bowl' for a surprising number of animals and plants. In human history north-eastern China is famous for the fierce tribe that left its forest homeland to ravage the eastern plains and carve out the Manchu Dynasty. But, zoologically, Manchuria has received many more invaders than it exported. The vagaries of climate and topography have produced a number of biological 'highways' along which animals and plants from almost every part of China have gained access to Manchuria's forests and plains, so that tropical species now mix incongruously with animals normally associated with arctic conditions. From the north come Siberian ground squirrels, pine martens, wolverine, the snowy owl and the decidedly curious racoon dog, a creature with remarkable powers of adaptation (including pseudo-hibernation, an ability unknown among other members of the dog family). The racoon dog has spread steadily across Eurasia and has recently reached as far west as Germany.

The great fastness of the Da Hinggan range merges with the eastern extensions of the Altai Mountains, allowing typically Himalayan species, such as rhododendron, Tibetan black bear (*Selenarctos thibetanus*) and ghoral (*Nemorhadeus goral*), to push their way almost to the Pacific Ocean. Above the treeline is alpine pasture and tundra with dwarf rhododendron and birches and their distinctive insect fauna. The mountains of the south are too low to have proved an effective barrier to invasion from the eastern plains of China. Long before the burgeoning human population of these agricultural flatlands exterminated much of the wildlife there, leopard, Bengal cat and parrotbirds had made the northward journey into the colder but by no means inhospitable Manchurian wilderness. As they did so, natural selection weeded out those less able to withstand the severe winter weather, favouring large size in order to conserve body heat; e.g. the Manchurian leopard (*Panthera pardis*) is over 3.75 m long, equal in size to the tigers of the south.

Despite its numerous immigrants, this natural zoological melting pot does boast some distinctive native species. The red-crowned crane is justly famous for its distinctive mating dance, the male and female springing together with wings extended and necks arched. The Manchurian tiger is by far the largest, and one of the rarest, of the world's big cats. Its broad, black and gold stripes break up its massive outline in the dappled light of the forest and the three black bars across its forehead, joined by a single vertical stripe, make the pictogram 'I', the Chinese character for King, and leave no doubt of its position in the forest hierarchy. Many plants, although familiar to Westerners, are found in north-eastern China in distinctive Manchurian varieties: Manchu oak, linden, hornbeam, maple, elm and the oddly named Manchurian Scots pine. Rare and endangered species include Hinggan fir (*Abies nephrolepis*) and Korean spruce (*Picea koraiensis*). In the understorey beneath the tree canopy are hazelnut, dogwood and roses, and climbers that are now familiar in gardens the world over: clematis and honeysuckle. In the Changbai Mountains the Chinese magnolia vine (*Schisandra chinensis*), now extremely rare, is also found.

But of all Manchuria's wild plants the ginseng is probably the rarest and most celebrated. And with good reason. In China its reputation goes back at least 2000 years to the *Canon of Materia Medica* of the Han Dynasty (*c.* 200BC). About 20 cm in height, with small flowers tinged yellow-green, all parts of the plant (but especially the root) are said to be endowed with almost magical properties of healing and health renewal, some of which have recently been vindicated by modern science. Ginseng grows on the forest floor and needs highly specialized growing conditions: indirect sunlight, cold temperatures during part of the year and damp but not waterlogged soil. It is most often found in the company of Korean pine, so often in fact that a folk tale has arisen to explain their apparent partnership.

Long ago, the ginseng lived in the Yimeng Mountains of Shandong Province (some 1000 km to the south of its present home). The ginseng married a Korean pine and their happiness was complete until a local warlord began cutting down the pines to build a new manor house. Terrified, the couple fled north to the Changbai Mountains where, because the ginseng was anxious in her new surroundings, her pine-husband pledged always to remain by her side.

But not one pine in a thousand has such a valuable 'wife'. The Chinese eschew cultivated forms of the root, and the wild variety is extremely rare, and treasured as a result. Fabulous prices are paid to the hunter lucky enough to stumble upon an exceptionally large root. Not that Manchurians believe that luck has anything to do with it. Such is the mystique that surrounds the ginseng, it is believed that only those of outstanding, unblemished character are vouchsafed a glimpse of the fabulous root. If greedy, wicked men search for the plant the root sinks back deeper into the earth, the mountains tremble, and another Manchurian inhabitant, Big Van, better known as 'the Manchurian tiger', comes forth to devour the miscreant.

Unfortunately, the true situation is quite the reverse. Scores of wetland habitats have been drained and turned over to cereal and soybean production. Though much progress has been made in the past decade, the forests are not yet managed on a sustainable basis. In many areas of Manchuria, people are in the process of 'devouring' the wilderness and with it the wildlife, including the few wild tigers that remain.

RED-CROWNED CRANE

THE CHINESE KNOW THE RED-CROWNED CRANE (*Grus japonensis*) AS THE 'IMMORTAL Crane' because it often appears in the company of Daoist immortals and bodhisattvas of ancient legend, sometimes carrying them through the air. For centuries it has featured in Chinese myth and folk tales along with the Siberian crane, the black-necked crane and others. The earliest reference to the 'Immortal Crane' appears in *Zuo Zhuan*, a book chronicling the history of the Spring and Autumn Period (eighth to fifth centuries BC). The story is told of Duke Yi of the state of Wei who was particularly fond of cranes. He treated them as honoured guests, allowing them to travel in carriages and even paying them. He

The red-crowned crane's (*Grus japonensis*) long, stilt-like
legs keep it high above the marshy ground and its long beak
is perfect for spearing fish.

accorded them the status of a high official, much to the annoyance of the Wei commanders and soldiers who complained during a campaign against the northern Di people: 'Since the cranes are so highly honoured, why not let them do the fighting?'

The song of the crane is referred to in the *Book of Songs*, the first collection of poetry in China dating back to the Western Chou Dynasty (1066–776 BC): 'The crying cranes in the marshes are heard up in the heavens.' So loud are their calls that they can be heard from 2 km away, their long necks and curving windpipes functioning like a French horn. Stretched out in flight, the slender necks and long legs present elegant silhouettes in formation. These willowy attributes serve the red-crowned crane well in feeding; the dagger-like beak and slender, flexible neck make it well adapted for striking fish and the long legs help the bird to wade through marshes, giving it an excellent viewpoint above the water when searching for fish.

The red-crowned crane is so called because both sexes have a distinctive, naked red crown. Male and female are almost indistinguishable as they are the same size and have the same body colouring. Adult birds are mostly pure white except for the deep black secondary and tertiary feathers, the dark brown cheeks, throat and neck, and the forehead and lores, which are sparsely covered with black feathers. When it is standing, the bird folds its wings over the white tail, giving the impression that the tail is black. Adult birds are about 1.3 m long and 7–9 kg in weight, and have a wingspan of about 150 cm.

RANGE A migratory species, the red-crowned crane breeds in the Ussuri Region of the Russian Federation, Korea, Japan, Inner Mongolia and Manchuria (Heilongjiang, Jilin and Liaoning Provinces) and overwinters in the Yangtze catchment area, particularly the famous reserve at Poyang Lake. The Japanese populations do not migrate. The main breeding grounds are the Wuyur and Qixing River Basins in Heilongjiang Province. This is largely due to a successful policy of protection and to a captive breeding programme at the reserve's research station. However, captive-bred birds reared here have lost the urge to migrate and stay put all the year round.

One of the world's most endangered cranes, the red-crowned crane on its breeding ground in Zhalong Marshes, Heilongjiang Province.

HABITAT The red-crowned crane depends on marshes and lakes for its livelihood. Chinese artists wrongly paint it perched on the branches of pine trees that actually occur in mountainous parts. Apart from this, a red-crowned crane would never be found perched on a tree. This artistic licence is used by the painter to show a double symbolism: the crane, a symbol of long life, juxtaposed with another well-known symbol of longevity, the Korean pine. A wildlife artist would have to paint the bird standing among sedge and reeds or wading in open water.

BEHAVIOUR Early in March, the cranes arrive in pairs or family groups from their winter feeding grounds in the south. So loud and sharp are their calls that the birds are usually heard before they are seen. They usually arrive to a very wintry scene. Large areas of reed and sedge are still trapped under thick layers of ice but the vice-like grip of winter is beginning to relax its hold even so. No time is lost in searching for mates and fights between males erupt as they vie for receptive females. Pairing is for life (the red-crowned crane is also a symbol of fidelity) so courtship is important in ensuring that male and female are compatible. The ritual takes the form of a rhythmic dance, the pair leaping and pirouetting around one another in excitement, stretching out their necks, and bowing and flapping their wings. They call out to each other as they dance and the duet often triggers a loud resonant chorus from other red-crowned cranes in the neighbourhood. As the excitement reaches fever pitch, the female bends her legs, opens her wings and moves her white tail feathers aside. The male responds by leaping onto the back of his partner and mating for several seconds.

Normally, offspring from the previous year will continue to stay close by but, once the pair have chosen a spot for nest-building, they will expel the yearling. These sub-adults tend to flock together until they reach sexual maturity 4 or 5 years later, when they pair off and live as couples away from the sub-adult flocks.

Both male and female help to make the nest, which is constructed on a mound of dried grass on flat open ground near water. A metre or so high and nearly 2 m in diameter, the nest is lined with reed leaves and catkins. The mated pair staunchly defend a territory of several sq.m. around the nest. The female normally lays two eggs, the first about 3 weeks after mating and the second a few days after the first and she does most of the incubating, depending on her mate to bring her food. The male also guards the nest against predators, such as hawks and weasels, that would make short work of eggs or chicks. The parents are aggressive and very vigilant during incubation and, for the last 2 or 3 days, the female does not even allow the male to do any of the incubating. After about 30 days, the chicks signal with cheeps that they are about to hatch and their mother does what she can to help them struggle free from the confines of the shell. This can take several hours but, once hatched, the chicks very soon leave the nest to start searching for food.

Freshly hatched chicks weigh about 150 gm and measure 220 mm or so in length. They are covered with soft down feathers of pale yellowish brown, the middle of their backs being slightly darker than their underparts. The base and middle parts of their bills are

cream-coloured and their sturdy toes are yellow-brown tinged with grey. The chicks stay close to their parents, both for protection and to learn the skills of hunting. Shrimps, aquatic insects and fish, such as crucian carp and loaches, are the main prey, supplemented with grasshoppers and the tender shoots of reeds and catkins. By the end of the summer the young birds are as proficient as their parents at catching their food.

Thirty-five days after hatching, the young birds have yellow-brown feathers on their shoulders and wings and their flight feathers are a dark brown. By 3 months of age, they have lost their down feathers and are very similar in colour to an adult although the whites and blacks are not yet quite as pure and the crown is still covered in short, dark brown feathers with no sign of a naked patch or red cap. Now almost fully grown, they start practising flight movements to strengthen their wing muscles, readying themselves for the 2500 km journey south. In late September to mid-October family groups leave the breeding grounds in flocks. These form an inverted 'V' formation as they wing their way to warmer climates.

The birds head for the middle and lower reaches of the Yangtze River. Their main wintering ground is Poyang Lake Nature Reserve in Jiangxi Province but some birds also flock to the smaller lakes and marshes in Anhui and Jiangsu Provinces. Poyang Lake is well known internationally. Great efforts have been made to protect the lake from the pressures that beset many of the neighbouring lakes, pressures such as rapid economic development and population growth, pollution from agricultural chemicals and over-hunting. Poyang attracts huge numbers of birds, many of which are rare species. Poyang Lake Bird Study Group has identified 150 species, of which 69 are on the protection list of the migrant birds preservation agreement (see p. 15) between China and Japan and 12 are protected by the Chinese Government. Migrants include whistling swans, Siberian, white-necked, common

A red-crowned crane chick at Zhalong Reserve, Heilongjiang.

and hooded cranes, white and black storks, mandarin ducks and bustards. The lake is approximately 65 km from east to west and 170 km from north to south.

Five rivers, the Gan, Fu, Xin, Yao and Xiushui, flow into Poyang Lake from the west, south and south-east and the lake then flows on into the Yangtze at Hukou. The five rivers enrich the lake with food and fish and bring a constant supply of silt that is deposited mainly at the mouth of the lake, forming sandbanks.

The climate at Poyang Lake is subtropical wet monsoon with a mean annual temperature of 17°C, the lowest winter temperatures being about 8°C. The frost period lasts for little more than 3 months of the year and the annual rainfall is 584 mm. The lake's water levels rise and fall sharply with the seasons. In the rainy season, from April to September, when migrant birds such as the red-crowned crane are busy breeding in their northern haunts, the lake covers an area of about 2800 km². It is an entirely different picture in the dry season, from October to March, when the migrants overwinter with their juvenile young. At this time of year the lake shrinks to just 500 km². Large expanses of muddy lake bottom and grassy islets appear and sand bars and mounds of earth divide the lake into numerous shallow ponds less than a metre in depth. Fish, shrimps and molluscs become concentrated in these ponds, providing easy pickings for the now swollen bird population.

The red-crowned cranes build up their reserves during this period and the juveniles mature into sub-adulthood. At 10 months of age, shortly before the northward flight, the young cranes start to acquire their red comb, albeit a duller red than that of their parents.

STATUS Nine of the world's 15 crane species occur in China and the red-crowned crane is one of the rarest. In May of 1981, 1984 and 1986, biologists from the Institute of Natural Resources in Harbin carried out aerial surveys of the red-crowned crane over the crane's breeding grounds in China. The biologists timed the surveys to coincide with the latter part of the bird's breeding season because the parent birds do not move from their nests then and so counting them is fairly straightforward at this time of year. The surveys covered over 4200 km² and were combined with ground surveys in both summer and winter sites. The biologists estimated a total population of 620 red-crowned cranes spread over eight main breeding sites in China (see table). The main breeding sites are the Wuyur River Basin in Zhalong Nature Reserve and the Qixing River Basin about 500 km to the east.

Numbers of red-crowned cranes in the eight main breeding grounds in China

Breeding ground	Number of cranes
Honghe Nature Reserve	51
Qixing River Basin	176
Lower reaches of Dulu River	23
Xingkai Lake	59
Wuyur River Basin	193
Hui River Basin	38
Lower reaches of Taoer River	50
Mouth of Shuangtaizi River	30
TOTAL	620

CONSERVATION MEASURES In China and also in Japan the red-crowned crane is legally protected. In 1981, the Governments of China and Japan signed the Agreement on the Conservation of Migratory Birds and their Habitats, which protects 227 species of birds that migrate between China and Japan. In China, the red-crowned crane and other crane species have been assigned six nature reserves within their breeding grounds, covering 4025 km². They are: Zhalong and Honghe Nature Reserves in Heilongjiang Province; Xianghai and Momoge Nature Reserves in Jilin Province; Shuangtaizihe Nature Reserve in Liaoning Province; and Yancheng Nature Reserve in Jiangsu Province.

Zhalong Nature Reserve is the main centre for research on cranes. It lies in the basin of the Wuyur River, a tributary of the Nen River. The swamps, lakes and reed beds scattered over the 420-km² area of the reserve also attract several other species of crane, among them common crane (*Grus grus*), demoiselle crane (*Anthropoides virgo*), Siberian crane (*G. leucogeranus*) and white-naped crane (*G. vipio*). Other rare species of water birds also take advantage of the prime feeding and breeding conditions. Zhalong is supported by a captive breeding-centre-cum-research-station where studies on bird behaviour and ecology are carried out. When we visited the area in 1984 and again in 1986 much research had been done on captive breeding of red-crowned crane (the original *raison d'être* for the reserve). This work has continued and many chicks have hatched. Unfortunately, whereas the wild cranes visiting the reserve migrate with the onset of winter to Poyang Lake and other wetlands in southern China, so far the captive-bred birds have failed to make the flight south.

But nature reserves and legislation do not guarantee protection on the ground and, in many parts of the northern reserves, villagers continue to cut reeds for the paper industry, depriving the red-crowned crane of nesting cover. Schaller writes of illegal hunting of various species of protected birds at Poyang Lake. The *China Daily* reported that during the winter of 1984–85 one village cooperative alone killed some 600 white storks, Siberian cranes, and whistling swans to make feather fans, and market hunters shot and poisoned about 200 000 wild fowl around the lake, despite a provincial ban against hunting. A public outcry finally brought some measure of protection. George Archibald of the International Crane Foundation has led enthusiastic tours of bird-watchers to both Zhalong and Poyang, illustrating the kind of benign economic use that should be promoted to benefit wildlife as well as local people.

MANCHURIAN TIGER

THE LARGEST OF ALL THE BIG CATS, THE TIGER (*Panthera tigris*) HAS A POWERFUL, muscular body covered in reddish/orange fur, except for the white underside, with broad, vertical black stripes along the flanks. The huge paws are armed with long, curved claws and the head is massive and rounded in shape. The eyes are yellow and the prominent ears are black in colour with a white central area front and back.

China is home to more subspecies of tiger than any other country. Four subspecies hunt within its borders: the Bengal tiger (*P. t. tigris*), the Indo-Chinese tiger (*P. t. corbetti*), the Manchurian tiger (*P. t. altaica*) and the south China tiger (*P. t. amoyensis*). While it is likely that, before the onset of agriculture, the ranges of the four subspecies overlapped to a greater or lesser extent, during the historical past human settlements, combined with geographical features such as mountains or rivers, have effectively separated them, allowing each to develop distinctive traits.

The largest of all the subspecies, the Manchurian tiger measures over 3.75 m from head to tail, weighs in at a massive 200 kg or more, and is characterized by its dense, long pelt, an adaptation to the intense cold of its natural home. The ground colour of the pelt is yellow and the white of the belly extends upwards onto the flanks. The tail is also white with just a trace of yellow at the base.

The Bengal tiger is the 'typical' tiger of India. The pelt is reddish/orange, sometimes almost brown, with dark and very prominent vertical stripes. The south China tiger is the only subspecies endemic to China. It is somewhat intermediary between the Manchurian and Bengal subspecies, with medium-long fur and a more vivid yellow ground colour to the pelt. Its stripes are also distinctive, regularly forming diamond-shaped patterns not normally seen in the other subspecies. At about 130 kg for a full-grown male it is the lightest of China's tigers. The Indo-Chinese tiger has many narrow stripes particularly close-set along the flanks. It was identified as a subspecies only in 1968.

RANGE The Bengal tiger, as its name implies, ranges into China from northern India (and Nepal) and inhabits southern Tibet (Xizang Autonomous Region) and part of western Yunnan. The Indo-Chinese tiger is, likewise, the northernmost expansion of its race (or perhaps more correctly the northernmost remnant of a formerly more extensive range) and is found in southern China's Yunnan Province, concentrated around the reserve of Xishuangbanna. The Manchurian tiger, if it has not already been hunted to extinction, seems to exist in two separate pockets. The first lies along the Heilong River (the border with the former USSR), notably in the Da and Xiao Hinggan ranges, and is contiguous with the remnants of the Siberian tiger population (which is the same subspecies). The second population centres around the Changbai range in south-eastern Jilin Province, and borders on the North Korean population of the Manchurian tiger. Although it is the most endangered

Opposite: The Manchurian tiger (*Panthera tigris altaica*) is the largest subspecies and ranges furthest north.

of all China's subspecies, the South China race has, ironically, the most extensive range. The animal can be found in Guangdong, Fujian, Jiangxi and Hunan Provinces, although in tiny numbers (see p. 40).

HABITAT The tiger is extremely adaptable and is not restricted to any particular habitat. It can be found in many different types of forest, from tropical mangrove through rainforest, dry forest and northern coniferous taiga where winter temperatures may fall as low as −40°C. In addition, tigers can hunt successfully in reed beds, elephant grass, and on mountains up to a height of 4000 m. As far as these diverse habitats are concerned, the tiger's main requirement is that they provide sufficiently tall and dense cover for the animal's hunting forays.

BEHAVIOUR All subspecies of tiger are solitary and they are normally found in groups only during the breeding season, when a mother is caring for her offspring, or, more rarely, when a number of siblings stay together for a brief period after leaving their mother. Tigers communicate with others of their species by means of calls and scent, spraying bushes and trees around their home range with a mixture of urine and secretions from the anal glands. As with leopards, pandas and many other carnivores, tree-scratching is also used as a means of indicating an individual's presence in its home range.

A tiger's home range can vary enormously, depending on the type of habitat over which it hunts. In Siberia, where prey is widely dispersed, territories of up to 3200 km^2 have been recorded, whereas an Indian tiger, with a more plentiful food supply, can make do with about 50 km^2. Spread throughout this territory a tiger has several lairs, usually under rocks or fallen trees, or in dense vegetation. The tiger uses the nearest den-site when hunting.

Prey comes in a bewildering assortment of species: everything from frogs, salmon and hare, through deer species, canids and gazelles, to tapir, rhinoceros and even elephant! In Manchuria, the tiger is known as 'Keeper of the Wild Boar', because of its habit of following boar packs and picking off the stragglers. Other prey includes locusts, buffalo, domestic cattle and, rarely, Man himself. When hunting, the tiger is capable of leaps of 5–6 m, to heights of almost 2 m. Prey is grasped in the jaws and, if small, despatched with a spine-crushing bite to the nape of the neck. Larger prey are seized by the throat and either asphyxiated or killed by snapping the vertebral column from below.

Despite its speed and size and ferocious aspect, a hunting tiger has a less than 50/50 chance of catching its chosen prey. The animal needs cover in order to move to within approximately 20 m of its chosen victim. For preference, the tiger will creep even closer, within 2–4 m, before overwhelming its prey with a sudden charge. If the intended victim avoids this initial onslaught, the tiger will pursue its prey for at most 200 m and then give up and begin again. The tiger needs to be persistent; it is a large animal and requires a substantial diet of meat to remain in good health. On average, a Bengal tiger consumes about 8 kg of meat a day, and the Manchurian tiger, being larger and living further north, requires even more. Nursing tigresses have an even higher requirement.

Tigers breed throughout the year but with a peak in late winter and spring. Male tigers' home ranges overlap with those of several females, and a tigress on heat will occasionally leave her own territory in search of a suitable mate. Gestation lasts 95–112 days and two to four young is the usual litter size. The cubs feed solely on their mother's milk for 2 months, after which meat slowly becomes a more important part of their diet. At around this time they first leave the birth-den and begin exploring their surroundings. They begin hunting alone at about 1 year old, although they will stay with their mother for 3 years (5 years for the Manchurian tiger). This extended care limits their breeding potential; a tigress will give birth only every 3–4 years (4–5 years in the Manchurian tiger).

STATUS All four subspecies are endangered within China but, in a global context, it is the Manchurian and the south China tigers that must cause greatest concern. There are believed to be a tiny number of Bengal tigers in western Yunnan and southern Tibet, probably fewer than ten animals. But this number is bolstered by the estimated 5000 Bengal tigers (and several conservation efforts) to be found across China's southern border in Nepal, India and Bangladesh. The Indo-Chinese subspecies is in a similar plight, with only about a dozen

When they are not actively hunting, Manchurian tigers spend much of their time resting.

animals, all in Yunnan Province's Xishuangbanna Reserve. Once again, neighbouring countries hold a much higher population, estimated at approximately 2000 animals.

Of the remaining two tigers, the Manchurian also has 'friends across the border' with Russia's Siberian tiger (which is the same subspecies) and the Manchurian tiger of North Korea numbering between 200 and 300 individuals. The Chinese Manchurian tiger population itself is tiny; estimates as high as 50 animals have been given recently, but the expansion of 'sport' hunting is believed by many to have drastically reduced even this tiny number. Some researchers believe the subspecies in China to be extinct in the wild. With between 200 and 350 animals living free internationally, time is not on the side of the Manchurian tiger.

The south China tiger is an even worse case. The subspecies is found only in China and there are no cross-border populations to help bolster the figures. Between October 1990 and February 1991, China's Ministry of Forestry and WWF-International sponsored a survey to determine the approximate number of south China tigers remaining in the wild. The results made poor reading. It is now believed that only a few dozen animals survive, spread over a huge area that includes Guangdong, Fujian, Hunan and Jiangxi Provinces. Incredibly, male and female tigers are still able to find one another in this vast area and, according to reports of hunters and others, reproduction is still occurring. Confirmation of this came tragically in the form of a 10-kg tiger cub which was run down on a road in Fujian Province in 1987.

Along with the depressingly familiar stories of logging and human agricultural expansion into previously untouched wilderness, two further factors have militated against China's tigers. The mass 'anti-pest' campaigns of the 1950s were mainly directed at perceived economic pests: rats, flies and mosquitoes were among the animals targeted. Many of these campaigns were misconceived, the most famous being the almost total destruction of sparrows in and around Beijing, in the mistaken belief that this would increase agricultural production. In fact, the opposite proved true and, without the sparrows to hold them in check, the numbers of insect pests increased dramatically. Less well known, but just as unwise, were anti-pest campaigns carried out in many remote areas: at one time or another bears, leopards and tigers were all marked down for destruction. In some cases these campaigns were simply the result of misplaced idealism; in others a pecuniary motive is likely. With a tiger carcass fetching over US $2000, and bears not much less, there is no doubt that such anti-pest drives were extremely lucrative for some unscrupulous bureaucrats. Of all the subspecies, the south China tiger suffered most and some experts date its almost terminal decline from the mass campaigns of the 1950s.

Alongside these sporadic campaigns has been the long-term demand for tiger carcasses for traditional medicines. The healing properties attributed to various organs of the tiger in Chinese medicine have played a major part in stimulating hunting. Tiger bones have long been used in the treatment of a variety of illnesses, including hemiplegia and joint sprains. Tiger urine was also said to be a sovereign remedy for rheumatism, although how this was obtained without the demise of the collector has never been satisfactorily explained!

CONSERVATION MEASURES The Chinese Government has various laws in place that should, in theory, protect the tiger. Unfortunately, despite many efforts, hunting and deforestation continue. While filming in Sichuan in 1993, we were personally offered a dried tiger's forepaw outside one of the main hotels in the provincial capital, Chengdu. The vendor was a middle-aged lady of one of the many minority groups of the south, and we can be confident that her 'merchandise' was an individual of the highly endangered south China tiger. Perhaps to counter this, the Chinese Government has put most of its resources into captive breeding efforts. This is a rather recent development and has tended to concentrate on the Manchurian tiger. The China Cat Family Species Breeding Centre, near Harbin in Heilongjiang Province has been attempting to breed the Manchurian tiger since 1986. According to the Xinhua News Agency, an original population of 22 animals has increased in 7 years to 62 and is projected to reach 300 animals by 1996. That the *raison d'être* for the centre is not purely conservation was shown in 1993 by China's formal application to CITES for the ban on trade in the tiger and its products to be lifted.

Such a concentration of resources on the Manchurian tiger is understandable when this subspecies is compared with the Bengal and Indo-Chinese tigers. These two races are still to be found in relatively high numbers in countries outside of China. But the reasons behind the lack of effort towards conserving the south China tiger, the one subspecies to be found only in China, are less obvious. The captive breeding effort here, such as it is, lacks coordination and commitment. A steering committee, The South China Conservation Coordination Group, set up in 1985, is now defunct. A survey in 1990 revealed that, of 17 Chinese zoos exhibiting south China tigers, ten possessed solitary animals, five had pairs, and Shanghai and Chongqing Zoos had eight animals (three males and five females) each. To compound the problem, in the past studbooks have been kept haphazardly, if at all, and the blood lines of many captive 'south China tigers' are suspect. In some cases this can be traced to the Shanghai Zoo's decision, in the early 1950s, to mate Manchurian tigers with those of the south China race. Unlike some other species (e.g. Przewalski's horse and Père David's deer), no viable breeding populations have been established outside of China. Of only six South China tigers sent abroad – two to Moscow Zoo (1952), two to Bucharest Zoo (1960s) and two males given as a 'gesture of friendship' to Sudan (1974) – all are dead.

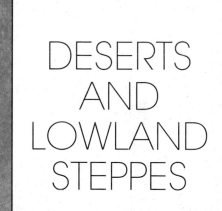

DESERTS
AND
LOWLAND
STEPPES

T HE DESERTS OF CHINA EXTEND OVER AN EIGHTH OF THE COUNTRY (MORE than 1 million km^2. They are found in the north-west, mainly in Xinjiang Uygur Autonomous Region but also in northern Qinghai and in parts of Gansu Province, Inner Mongolia (Nei Mongol Autonomous Region) and Tibet (Xizang Autonomous Region). About 60 per cent are sandy; the remainder are stony deserts. It is an ecosystem hostile to life, intensely hot during the day and often cold during the night, and very dry. Annual rainfall in a year ranges from 6 mm to less than 200 mm. Huge daily and annual variations in temperature add to the challenge of survival, and winds of up to 120 k.p.h. intensify these swings between bitter cold and searing heat. In the face of such winds the desert literally moves. Huge sand dunes rapidly disappear, whipped into sandstorms, and re-appear elsewhere so that there are few permanent landmarks by which a traveller can navigate. Until fairly recently, human presence was limited to a handful of nomadic tribes of Turkic origin that made their living from livestock, shifting home with the seasons. Today, some people still lead a traditional nomadic life, but irrigation with groundwater and special breeds of livestock and grasses have encouraged many settlements. Ranching and even the cultivation of arable crops are now possible. The exploration of oil, minerals and salt have drawn immigrants here from other parts of China and have added to the pressures on wildlife living in the region.

A small leaf area is a feature of many indigenous plant species, e.g. peashrubs (*Caragana* spp.) which have tiny leaves; various kinds of wormwood (*Seriphidrum* and *Artemisia* spp.), which have deeply divided and fingered leaves; broom-like shrubs of the genus *Calligonum* and the salt-tolerant *Anabasis*, which have slender, stiff leaves. The common horaninowia (*Horaninowia ulicinia*) and leafless *Anabasis* (*A. aphylla*) are almost leafless and rely on the new growth of green branches for photosynthesis. The leaves of other plants reduce water loss by rolling up during the hottest part of the day, e.g. fescue grasses (*Festuca* spp.) and feather or needle grasses (*Stipa* spp.).

Other ways of reducing water loss are to have a covering of fine hair or a thick cuticle, or fewer stomata in the leaves. Many salt-tolerant plants, e.g. goosefoot, fat hen (*Chenopodium album*) and kalidium (*Kalidium gracile*) contain a salty sap which is an

Previous page: The desert region of northern Qinghai, bereft of all plant cover.

Above: The reduced leaves of many desert plants help to conserve moisture.

effective dump for soluble salts. *Reaumuria* spp. and the closely related Tamarisk (*Tamarix* spp.), which help stabilize dunes, expel salt through their stomata, and their leaves and stems have a waxy layer to conserve moisture. During prolonged drought they will shed their leaves, or even their branches, becoming dormant until the next rainfall. Saxauls (*Haloxylon* spp.), are also important in binding sand dunes. They grow to 1–3 m tall and are densely branched. Once the dunes have 10–20 per cent plant cover, they stabilize and other plants take over.

The desert fauna is limited to those species that can withstand the hostile climate and a landscape that is short on food and cover. Many species of the Qinghai-Tibet Plateau manage to live in these deserts but the ungulates tend to live in the less barren areas where there is suitable plant food. Among them is the two-humped Bactrian camel (*Camelus bactrianus*), which used to have a wide distribution in Xinjiang, Gansu and Qinghai but is now rare and limited to just a few of its old haunts. Bactrian camels feed on the leaves of tamarisks, saxauls, poplars and others. They can live for a month without water by storing reserves in the fat of their hump. Herds of Przewalski's gazelle (*Procapra przewalskii*) live in the low hills and stony desert and feed on tender leaves and shoots of desert plants. The species is in decline because of hunting and deterioration of its habitat but its relative, the goitered gazelle (*Gazella subguttorosa*), is even worse off because it is now believed to be extinct in China. Rodents and reptiles are the most common animal groups as they are the best adapted to desert conditions. The predominant rodents are jerboas and gerbils which cope by being nocturnal, remaining in their burrows during the scorching heat of the day. The majority of reptiles are lizards but there are also desert snakes and one species of tortoise. Birds are less well represented but those that live here have evolved various means of dealing with their environment. They pant and ruffle their feathers to cool themselves and, during the hottest hours of the day, parent birds often stand over their eggs to shade them. Black-bellied sandgrouse (*Pterocles orientalis*) use an insulating pocket under the skin as a heat shield to protect against reflected light. Sandgrouse fly long distances to drink at a regular time of day and the males can transport water to their chicks in their absorbent belly feathers. Large birds of prey are rare and the only ones that are seen in the deserts, hunting rabbits and rodents, are the long-legged buzzard (*Buteo rufinus*) and booted eagle (*Hieraaetus pennatus*). The European or blue roller (*Coracias garrulus*) is much more common, as is the Isabelline wheatear (*Oenanthe isabellina*) and desert wheatear (*O. deserti*). Many summer visitors fly into the desert to feed on plant and insect food, and reptiles and rodents. They include the desert warbler (*Sylvia nana*), desert lark (*Ammomanes deserti*), stone curlew (*Burhinus oedicnemus*), pallid harrier (*Circus macrourus*) and shrikes (*Lanius* spp.).

China's deserts are found in several inland basins and plateaux at an altitude of 500–3000 m, ringed by mountains that rise to over 4000 m. There is the huge Tarim Basin, the Qaidam Basin and the Junggar Basin. *Qaidam* means 'salt' in Mongolian and most of the Qaidam Basin was actually a salt-lake which evaporated, leaving a lifeless plain of salt. The few small salt-lakes that dot the centre of the basin are all that is left to remind us of the

Overleaf: Desert plants, although they are sparse, help to stabilize sandy soils.

original lake. The crust of salt is 15 m thick in some parts and the very homes of the people that help mine the salt are made out of the mineral. Despite the inimical conditions the edge of the plateau is cultivated in a few places where there is a cover of wind-blown loess and where streams, fed by meltwater from the mountain snows, provide moisture for crops.

The Tarim Basin is characterized by a large central sandy desert, the Taklimakan Desert (327 000 km^2 in area) and an outer stony/sandy desert at the foot of the surrounding mountains. In between is a stony belt covered in parts with soil and interspersed with oases. Conditions are so hot here (sand temperatures of 84°C have been recorded) that rainwater evaporates before reaching the ground. Life is a struggle against an unforgiving climate and *Taklimakan* means 'the place of no return'. Unlike higher altitude deserts, such as the Taxkorgan Desert in south-western Tibet, it never gets cold at night because the surrounding mountains act as storage heaters, absorbing heat during the day and radiating it out after sunset. When the skies darken over it is not with rain clouds but with sandstorms. *Tarim* in the Uygur language means 'the converging of rivers' and, in fact, the only water of any significance comes from the rivers that cross the basin. It is these that support oasis-type plants, such as poplars (*Populus* spp.) and occasional Siberian elm (*Ulmus pumila*), and make the growing of cereals and cotton viable, but growth is limited to the river banks, creating ribbons of contrast between green foliage and yellow desert. The Tarim River, the longest inland river in China, flows through the Taklimakan Desert but eventually dries up in the Lop lowland, the lowest point of the desert which lies to the east. It used to flow into Lop Nur Lake but water diversions for agriculture in the middle and lower reaches of the river made the lake retreat until it finally disappeared in about 1970. What remains are large deposits of alkali, gypsum and salt sand blasted into strange shapes by the desert wind.

The Junggar Basin, the second largest desert in China, is in the far north-western corner of China and extends for 47 300 km^2. A cool north-westerly wind brings twice the amount of rain as in the Tarim and this is enough to support a denser plant cover which stabilizes the sand dunes and is used for winter grazing. The cool winds also produce winter temperatures as low as −20°C. The southern edge of the basin at the foot of the Tien Mountains features good soils and plentiful water, conditions which have produced fertile plains.

China's other major deserts are the Axla Desert of western Inner Mongolia and the Ordos Desert south of the huge U-bend of the Yellow River (Huang He). The prevailing north-westerly winds push the desert further to the south-east every year and cover roads, railways and crops. Efforts to plant trees and grass help to reduce the trend.

China's lowland steppes occur mostly as a broad belt on the Inner Mongolian Plateau running from the eastern foot of the Qilian Mountains north-east to the Da Hinggan Mountains. The plateau is an ancient one, eroded through its history to a characteristic flat table 1000–1300 m high. The climate here is not as harsh as in the high steppe zones of the Qinghai-Tibet Plateau. Cold and windy, the winters are not much different but the summers are warmer and bring the 'extra' rain that produces the very tall grasses typical of this region. This is largely due to the influence of the Pacific monsoon which, while much weakened by the time it reaches the plateau, is sufficient to bring 350 mm or so of rain each year. The effect of the monsoon gradually lessens the further west one travels and the low steppe gradually downgrades to desert. Livestock farming is important in the region, particularly in the east, where the grasses grow so tall that, on a day with little wind, it is not possible to see domestic cattle or wild herds of grazing Mongolian gazelle (*Procapra gutturosa*).

Grasses are the dominant plant in lowland steppe. There is a greater amount of needle or feather grass (*Stipa orientalis*), which likes well-drained, limey soils, Krylov's needle grass (*S. krylovii*), June grass (*Koeleria cristata*) and crested wheatgrass (*Agropyron cristatum*). Vetches and various other species are also found growing within the wide expanses of grasses. In the drier parts of this zone, vegetation is much sparser and consists mainly of perennial herbs with some tough, low bushy shrubs, all adapted to long, dry periods and intermittent rain. The most common species are Gobi needle grass (*S. gobica*), short-flowered needle grass (*S. breviflora*) and sandy needle grass (*S. glareosa*).

The Mongolian gazelle is a typical ungulate of China's lowland steppes. In good pastures, it may form large herds of up to several dozen animals, grazing on forage grasses and migrating with the seasons. Very successful inhabitants are the small mammals, such as rodents and lagomorphs. Many of them live in large groups with complex underground burrow systems and their numbers fluctuate with the seasons. Among them are pikas, hares, the Bobak marmot (*Marmota bobak*), hamsters and zokors. Birds, reptiles and amphibians are not numerous here. The birds are represented by larks, sandgrouse (Pteroclidae), lapwings and magpies, and the larger species include the great bustard (*Otis tarda*), steppe or tawny eagle (*Aquila rapax*) and rooks (*Corvus frugilegus*).

The loess plateau is included in the low-steppe vegetation zone, although today the original grassland and forest covers have long since been removed. Loess is dust that originated 2 million years ago from deserts in the north-west and was blown here by the prevailing winds. Long exposure to rain has turned it into a porous yellow-brown soil that is rich in nitrogen, phosphorus and potassium. It is nearly 200 m deep in many places on the plateau. Early settlers recognized the natural fertility of the soil and replaced the natural vegetation with their crops. Because the soil's fine texture makes it very susceptible to wind erosion when dry, and easy to wash away in summer rainstorms, the result has been serious degradation of the land.

People continue to work the soil to this day and even make their homes out of it. A journey by bus from Lanzhou to Xining took us through this strange landscape of bare, yellow earth. It was our first experience of the cave houses we had read so much about. The smoke of domestic fires issued from holes in the roofs and we saw women sweeping the floors in the constant battle to keep out the dust. We could only be impressed by the way these people took advantage of the natural properties of the earth. The loess walls are excellent insulation against the outside temperature, keeping the occupants warm in winter and cool in summer.

PRZEWALSKI'S HORSE

THE ONLY REMAINING TRULY WILD HORSE IN EXISTENCE, PRZEWALSKI'S HORSE (*Equus przewalski*) is about the size of a large pony but more heavily built (weight is 250–300 kg; shoulder height 124–145 cm), with a relatively larger head and a powerful jaw with strong masseter (cheek) muscles, especially in the male. The ears are small and pointed and the upper lip is somewhat longer than the lower and sometimes overlaps it. The neck is short, broad and very muscular, with a 'toothbrush' mane but no forehead tuft as in domestic horses. The back is short and normally straight and the deep, powerful chest makes the legs appear rather short, although they are not thick-set.

Foals of Przewalski's horse are born with a bright, yellow-brown coat. By the end of their first season this has become a brownish to reddish yellow, the belly much lighter in colour and the legs brown or black, with stripes around the carpal region (a characteristic of all primitive equids). The area around the mouth is almost pure white and a narrow white ring usually surrounds the eye.

In winter, the fur becomes much denser and longer because, unlike domestic horses, Przewalski's horse has only a single moult, but new hairs grow twice annually. Instead of the autumn shedding which is usual in other animals, Przewalski's horse grows additional hairs at this time. These hairs are sometimes 10 cm long and thicken the summer coat, making the pelt much denser and able to withstand the biting winter weather. The hairs are of a lighter hue, almost certainly an adaptation to the snow-covered environment.

RANGE Now localized in areas of the Trans-Altaic Gobi between China and south-western Mongolia, this species formerly ranged from the Mongolian steppes west to Kazakstan and the Urals. In China, Gao and Gu (1989) were unable to find any sign of Przewalski's horse 'though we have surveyed (for) it for years'. They believe, nevertheless, that the wild horse may still survive in small numbers in the 10 000 km² of desert–steppe to the east of Mount Beitashan on the border with Mongolia. However, many authorities believe the species to be extinct in the wild.

HABITAT Salt steppe and semi-desert, at 1000–1400 m above sea level, are the home of this horse. The vegetation here is poor, comprising almost exclusively halophilous (salt-loving) plants such as saxaul (*Haloxylon ammodendron*), wormwood (*Artemisia incana*) and feather grass (*Stipa orientalis*). The horses were also said to inhabit mountain areas at an altitude of up to 2000 m. Here the vegetation is even poorer, mainly species of grasses such as *Stipa*, *Agropyron*, *Festuca*, where the ground phytomass yield was 2.95 Calories/ha or above (Sokolov *et al.*, 1991). Even during its heyday, the species was not found in the extremely arid, bushy and semi-bushy desert types. In true deserts Przewalski's horses could be found only around oases.

BEHAVIOUR Much of this species' behaviour has probably been altered in recent years to mitigate the effects of hunting by human beings – the animal's activities before the advent of Man were probably somewhat different. They are said to graze during dusk and early morning, and to leave their feeding and watering sites at sun-up to spend the whole of the day in the desert. When drinking, mares with foals are allowed to satisfy themselves first, followed by unaccompanied mares and juveniles. The stallion drinks last.

Przewalski's horses live in small herds (harems) composed of a lead stallion, females and young. Most sightings in the wild report herd size to be no greater than 20 individuals. In captivity, the lead stallion remains 7–20 m from the other members of the herd, who watch him constantly, even while feeding. If attacked, the herd usually flees, the stallion bringing up the rear and often charging intruders. When the herd contains no foals, the stallion is less concerned, and holds a position at the side of the herd. For predators other than humans, e.g. wolves, another defensive strategy is employed: Przewalski's horses stand in a more or less closed circle, their heads facing inwards, with the young foals at the centre.

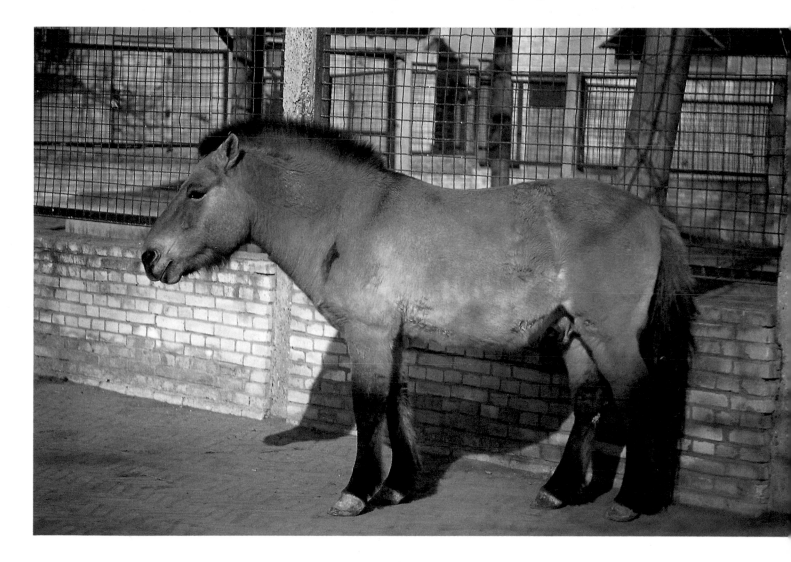

Captive Przewalski's horses (*Equus przewalski*) are now the only hope of saving this unique species of wild equiid.

Any predators approaching too close (bear and wolf are the main danger) have to contend with a continuous line of flashing hooves. This formation is also assumed during winter blizzards (the foals in the centre of the circle enjoying a temperature several degrees warmer than that of the air outside the circle), and in the height of summer, when plagues of flies can make life intolerable for the horses. The mass of waving tails acts as a giant fly-whisk, keeping the troublesome insects at bay! The animals also run in a chain, each horse benefiting from the fly-repelling tail beats of the horse in front.

Mating depends upon climate but, in Prague Zoological Garden, the mares come into heat between May and July, usually for 2–4 days. Competition for females between the stallions can lead to bloody fights, the rivals biting and kicking viciously with their forelegs. Each stallion tries to seize its opponent, throw him to the ground and kill or incapacitate with a bite to the nape of the neck. In Prague, foals are dropped from mid-April to mid-July. As she approaches term, the female keeps aloof from other herd members. The foal is often born at night, the mother licking the newborn and guarding it from all-comers with bites and kicks. The female Przewalski's horse is normally sexually mature at between 3 and 5 years of age, the male a year or two later.

STATUS Przewalski's horse represents the final survivor of a holocaust that has continued over many hundreds of years. Only 300–400 years ago this species, represented by at least three separate subspecies, roamed the forests and plains across the whole of Eurasia, from eastern Mongolia to the steppes and forests of central Europe as far west as Poland. In central Europe the creature was known as the 'tarpan', and there were distinct forest (*E. p. silvaticus*), and steppe-land (*E. p. gmelini*) subspecies. However, a rapid expansion of the human population, combined with increasing technological/agricultural sophistication (mirrored now by events in many parts of the developing world), led to deforestation and agricultural expansion on an enormous scale and, by the end of the eighteenth century, the forest tarpan was considered extinct. The plains tarpan lasted a little longer, disappearing during the nineteenth century.

The eastern subspecies was not known to exist at this time. It was discovered in 1879 by the famous Russian explorer Nikolai Mikhailovich Przewalski, in Kobdo, Mongolia. Although unable to obtain a live specimen, Przewalski did bring back both a skull and skin of the new animal. This physical evidence finally confirmed the existence of these wild horses, whose presence had been suspected for years. For example, in 1814, Cossacks serving in the occupation of Paris had told a British army officer that wild horses were to be found in Mongolia, and Przewalski himself had claimed a sighting of these creatures during his first expedition, 9 years earlier. In 1881 the taxonomist, Polyakov, gave this new horse species its scientific name, *Equus przewalski*, in honour of its discoverer.

Since then, the story of this last wild horse has been one of steady decline. Hunting, plus inexorable encroachment on the last of its grazing areas, pushed the wild horse into increasingly more marginal habitat, the driest and least hospitable areas of desert steppe. While there is just a chance that a few wild horses survive in the wild, it is generally believed that the animal is extinct in its natural environment. Fortunately (though by no means intentionally) animals caught in the late 1800s and early 1900s have proved to be the saviours of the species, at least in captivity. Altogether about 53 animals were captured during this period, many of them (39) for Carl Hagenbeck's zoo in Hamburg.

CONSERVATION MEASURES The initial breeding base from which the remaining 500 or so Przewalski's horses have sprung amounts to no more than 12 of the wild-caught ancestors that made their way to Europe in the latter part of the nineteenth and the early twentieth century. The stock is therefore extremely inbred. Deleterious effects of such a small genetic base are likely to become apparent and, unless great care is taken in the choice of breeding partners, the population may not be viable in the long term. In addition, the remaining animals are spread over more than 80 zoos and animal parks and the logistical problems in transferring individuals between all these establishments, so as to maximize genetic variability, are considerable.

In 1960, Prague Zoological Garden took the first step in overcoming this problem by establishing a studbook, recording the worldwide location of all specimens of Przewalski's horse. In 1972, the studbook showed more than 200 individual animals, four times as many as in 1958, and the number has risen steadily since then, to about 500 horses.

WWF France have taken the next obvious step with a long-term project which began in 1982. The scheme envisages the establishment of six reserves in the Netherlands and France especially designed for breeding Przewalski's horses under natural conditions. The first semi-reserve to begin work was in Lelystad Nature Park, where the State Service for the Ijssel Lake Polders, in conjunction with Amsterdam Zoo, have provided land to establish the project. The second reserve has been established by the Netherlands' State Forestry Commission, which has provided 1500 ha on and around the Veluwe River. Both these areas have been stocked with harem groups (of females plus stallion). In addition, five stallions, available for breeding with any group of Przewalski's horses worldwide, is kept near the city of Nijmegen in a 100-ha enclosure.

The hope is that all these reserves will greatly boost genetic diversity within the remaining population of Przewalski's horses, and that it will prove possible, eventually, to re-introduce some of these animals into the wild in their native land.

Such a possibility increases daily. A herd of Przewalski's horses has been established in a desert enclosure in the Junggar Basin in northern Xinjiang. Composed of 16 captive-bred animals, they are thriving in a 500-ha, walled enclosure. It is hoped that they will increase to at least 80 animals, at which point some may be released to fend for themselves. A second captive herd, in Gansu Province, is also earmarked for future release into the wild. As with most captive breeding projects, the critical factor is whether there will be any wilderness left into which the animals may be released. The wild horses' needs are very specific. Work done in the former USSR by Sokolov and his co-workers (Sokolov *et al.*, 1991) prompted these researchers to warn that: 'the project of restoring *Equus przewalski* . . . should be confined to its historic range.'

BACTRIAN CAMEL

THE DOMESTIC BACTRIAN CAMEL WITH ITS TWO HUMPS IS WELL-KNOWN TO MOST people from travel and adventure books on central Asia. But, while the skeletons of wild and domestic Bactrian camels are virtually indistinguishable, the wild camel (*Camelus bactrianus*) is both leaner and meaner compared to the human-friendly variety. Domestic camels are thick-set animals with large irregularly shaped twin humps and long shaggy coats of a predominantly dark brown hue. By contrast, the wild camel's humps are of only modest size and are invariably conical in shape. Their coat is short and sandy to grey-brown in colour and they are far more lightly built than their domestic cousins, weighing about 450–500 kg, with a total body height (excluding head and neck) of 2 m.

RANGE Less than 1000 years ago, the wild camel could lay claim to a range extending from Kazakhstan in the west, eastwards for over 3000 km to the Ordos Desert in the great

Like the yak, Bactrian camels have long been domesticated.

bend of the Yellow River (Huang He) of north-central China's Shaanxi Province. According to Bannikov (1976), by the 1850s, hunting had reduced its range to the western Gobi Desert on the borders of Mongolia and China and to the Taklimakan Desert of China's Xinjiang Uygur Autonomous Region, where it was 'discovered' in 1877 by the Russian explorer, Nikolai Mikhailovich Przewalski. The range has slowly declined since then. Tulgat and Schaller (1992) estimate the present total range to be around 155 000 km². At present the species can be found in Xinjiang and in Gansu Province in China, with a separate population existing to the north-east, across the border in Mongolia. The Chinese population is thought to number around 500 animals, focused around the Lop Nur region, principally to the north-east, east and south-east of the (now desiccated) lake. The eastern-most extension of their Chinese range is in western Gansu (Cheng, 1984). Its westerly extension is not known but isolated herds may exist as far west as Yutian in the Tarim Basin.

In Mongolia, a similar number of wild camel (i.e. a further 500 animals) is to be found in the Great Gobi National Park.

HABITAT The Taklimakan Desert is a forbidding place, consisting of a mixture of sun-baked plains littered with stone rubble and sand deserts dominated by shifting dunes. The area suffers a continental climate with extremes of temperature and very little rain. Nevertheless, the region is almost completely ringed by mountains. From these, numerous rivers, fed by snow-melt, drain into the Taklimakan to be swallowed up in the desert sands. While they remain above ground, these freshwater courses provide moisture for dense stands of tall grasses, such as *Phragmites communis* (a type of sedge), tamarisk (*Tamarix* spp.) and cottonwood (*Populus*), perfect food for the wild camel. In the Gobi or Mongolia, the land is less sandy, with wide barren plains of pebble-covered rock lying between mountain blocks, such as the Atas Ula and Chingis Ula, which rise to about 2100 m and more. *Phragmites* spp. and other grasses flourish at the few oases, but the bulk of the desert is devoid of grass, with only low shrubs, e.g. saxaul (*Haloxylon ammodendron*), and *Sarsola arbuscula*, adapted to drought conditions. It is these shrubs which form the bulk of the camel's diet in this region.

BEHAVIOUR Although a small number of animals of both sexes are solitary, the majority of wild camel live in herds, numbering, on average, between five and six individuals. The largest herd seen in China over the last ten years numbered 23 animals whereas, in Mongolia, about 6–10 per cent of all camels live in herds of 30 or more. Herd size varies with the season, being largest during the driest season (May to November), when the camels spend most of their time around their desert drinking places. Larger herds are also more frequent during the rut, the first signs of which (male to male combat) begin towards the end of November.

The rut is at its peak for about 1 month, from the end of January to the end of February. During this time each male tries to gather together a 'harem' of as many females as he can manage, with whom he mates and from whom he chases any other approaching male. As the

Overleaf: A domesticated camel herd in Qaidam Basin.

male:female sex ratio is of the order of 1:1.5, and as successful males may gather together a harem of up to 20 females, there are many males looking to topple the harem-owner. Weaker challengers are chased off but, if more evenly matched, the two males will engage in fierce battles 'often terminating in the death of one or other of the combatants' (Przewalski, 1879). Birth of young occurs more than 12 months later, in March and early April, the wild camel mirroring the domestic camel's long gestation period of 406 days. The gravid female loses her herding instinct and becomes solitary, abandoning the rest of the group and seeking out lower, warmer climes in which to give birth to her young, usually a single calf. It is a further 2 weeks before female and infant rejoin the herd. Young camels can travel almost as soon as they are born, an adaptation which makes them less vulnerable to wolves and other predators.

Wolves appear to be the only major predator of wild camel. Over a 5-year period in the Gobi Desert population, R. Tulgat, a Mongolian researcher, discovered 89 dead camel. Of these some 61 per cent were killed by wolves (*Lupus canis*), 2 per cent by snow leopard (*Panthera uncia*), 9 per cent by poachers and 12 per cent were due to injuries resulting from male to male fights during the rut. The cause of death could not be determined for the remaining 16 per cent of kills (Tulgat & Schaller, 1992). In almost all cases, young, juvenile, old or sick animals had been the wolves' targets. Tulgat and Schaller believe that wolf predation may have a significant effect on the camel population during periods of drought. When the rains fail, forage becomes dry and desiccated and the camels are unable to obtain sufficient water from plants alone. As a result, they need to drink more often. This effectively confines the herd to the areas around oases, which may in turn make the camels more vulnerable to wolf attack. Drought may also reduce the numbers of alternative prey, such as argali (*Ovis ammon*) and goitered gazelle (*Gazella gutturosa*), forcing the wolves to concentrate their efforts more on the camel as potential prey.

STATUS Neolithic sites over 6000 years old contain camel bones which may be the first evidence of hunting of this species by humans. Hunting has been the major source of the wild camel's decline over the past 1000 years and, in Mongolia, still accounts for almost 10 per cent of all deaths. During the past decade, the Mongolian wild camel population of the Great Gobi National Park seems to have fluctuated between 400 and 600 animals. However, the data presented by Tulgat and Schaller reveals a species still in gradual decline. Survival rates for young camel were low and recruitment into the population was less than that required to replace those losses from the adult population due to predation, poaching and simple old age. In the 8 years of the census (1982–1989), only in one year (1988) was the number of surviving young sufficient to compensate for 'natural wastage' in the camel population as a whole. This enormous attrition on young camel may be due to the drought that presently afflicts the region (see above) and culling of wolves has been instituted in an attempt to reduce predation pressure to tolerable limits (118 wolves were destroyed between 1987 and 1989). If this measure proves successful, it may be that the camel population of the Mongolian Gobi will return to something approaching stability.

In China the camel's status is far less clear and its future less certain. No systematic survey of the species' range and numbers has yet been undertaken and we cannot even guess at the survival rates for young camel. Even 100 years ago it was rare. Przewalski wrote:

Twenty years ago wild camels were numerous near Lake Lob. . . . Our guide told us that it was not unusual in those days to see some dozens, or even a hundred of these animals together. He himself had killed upwards of a hundred of them in the course of his life, with a flint-and-steel musket. With an increase of population . . . the hunters of Lob-Nor became more numerous and the camels scarcer. Now the wild camel frequents only the neighbourhood of Lob-Nor, and even here in small numbers. Years pass without so much as one being seen.

Today, all available evidence points to the conclusion that, as in the Gobi, the wild camel in China is still in decline. With motorized transport now readily available, hunters can travel far into the desert in search of prey, and camel meat is highly esteemed. In addition, human expansion in the region is continuing and new settlements quite naturally spring up around oases, the only sources of water for Man and beast in this parched landscape. With most water sources 30–40 km apart, if even one becomes unavailable to the camels it means a longer, more arduous, perhaps even fatal trek between drinking places. Sven Hedin's comment that camels 'shun every place that human beings visit, however seldom' has proven disastrously true and this behavioural trait, together with people's apparently insatiable desire for land, is forcing the wild camel further into marginal habitat.

CONSERVATION MEASURES China has designated two camel reserves. The first, established in 1982, is the Annanba Nature Reserve in Gansu Province; the second, in Xinjiang Autonomous Region, is the Altun Mountain Reserve, which was established in 1986. Together, the two reserves comprise an area of over 19 000 km². Additional research is needed in both these areas to discover population size and distribution of the reserves' wild camel. Trained staff are also required to help police the area and to enforce the strict protection conferred upon the wild camel by Chinese law. The Great Gobi National Park in Mongolia has six personnel who patrol the northern and central sections of the park regularly but, with such a wide area to cover, the protection afforded the camel is not satisfactory. The southern segment of the park, close to the border with China, is apparently seldom visited. The Mongolian authorities have also begun a captive breeding programme (established in 1987). The plan is to bring together a breeding group of 20 animals, which it is hoped will produce surplus animals for future release back into the wild.

One conservation problem that neither the Chinese nor the Mongolian authorities seem to have adequately addressed is the question of dilution of the wild camel gene pool by domestic stock. Domestic and wild Bactrian camel readily hybridize and the proximity of nomadic pastoralists and their herds to the wild populations must pose a constant threat to the genetic integrity of the wild camel. In the Great Gobi National Park culling of obvious hybrids has taken place several times, but the real answer must be the separation of all wild and domestic herds.

QINGHAI-TIBET
PLATEAU:
UPLAND
STEPPES

I N THE FAR DISTANT PAST, THE REGION THAT WAS TO BECOME THE QINGHAI-TIBET
Plateau was low-lying and part of the area was actually submerged below the waters of
the Tethys Ocean. But 40 million years ago, a literally earth-shattering event changed
everything. In its inexorable movement northwards, the Earth's Indo-Australian plate
was brought up against the Eurasian land mass. The northernmost edge of the Indian
subcontinent (which at that time was wholly separate from any other land mass) smashed
against Eurasia and was subducted (forced beneath) the larger plate, the crustal elements
being scoured from it as it went. The double layer of crust (Eurasian and Indian) was
crushed and folded, pushing ever skyward to form the world's highest mountain range – the
Himalayas. The land to the north of the Himalayas was also affected by this momentous
event and, as it rose, the Tethys Ocean shrank away westwards and eventually formed the
Mediterranean Sea. The mountain-building process is still ongoing; Mount Everest
(Qomolangma) is rising by an average of a few centimetres per year.

It is hard to imagine the size and altitude of this vast super-upland, which comprises
a total area of 2.2 million km². The Qinghai-Tibet Plateau's present average elevation is
4000 m, while Mont Blanc, the highest mountain in Europe, is a mere 4870 m. And this
is only the plateau height; the surrounding mountains tower 2000–3000 m higher. Oxygen
levels are low and so is air pressure (water boils at only 80°C). Travellers are likely to
suffer from mountain sickness, an extremely serious condition for those not properly

Previous page: 'The roof of the world': the Qinghai-Tibet Plateau.

Above: Peaks of eternal ice and snow: mountains on the edge of
the Qinghai-Tibet Plateau.

acclimatized to these conditions. During a visit to China in 1986, we learnt that a colleague of ours, on a filming expedition in Qinghai to cover a USA/China raft race down the Yangtze River, had collapsed and died from mountain sickness.

To the north, the Altun and Qilian ranges run east to west and effectively divide Qinghai from the low-lying desert wastes of Xinjiang Uygur Autonomous Region. To the west lie the Karakoram and Kunlun Mountains while, in the east, a tangled mass of minor ranges run in a confusing array down towards the Province of Sichuan. Forming the southern boundary of the Qinghai-Tibet Plateau are the Himalayas, the tallest of the world's mountain ranges. The average elevation of the Himalayas is a mighty 6220 m, but even this is dwarfed by the 8848-m peak of Mount Everest.

The high peaks in the east of the Qinghai-Tibet Plateau are the source of four of eastern Asia's mightiest rivers. The Yellow River (Huang He) runs almost directly east, picking up the vast amounts of yellow silt that give the river its name, and discharging it into the Bo Sea off Shandong Province, 5464 km from its source. The remaining rivers, the Nu, the Lancang and the Jinsha, follow the line of mountains down from the Tanggula to the Hengduan Mountains, where they form parallel courses, each just a few hundred kilometres from one another but entirely separated by the high peaks between. Once through the mountains, the Jinsha River turns east to become the Yangtze River (Chang Jiang), greatest of all the Middle Kingdom's watercourses. The Yangtze runs for 6300 km across the breadth of China while the other rivers continue south, the Nu as the Salween and the Lancang as the Mekong River, two of the major waterways of South-East Asia.

The southern slopes of the Himalayas catch almost the full content of the south-west monsoon. Part of southern Tibet (Xizang Autonomous Region) benefits from this high precipitation with annual rainfall up to 1000 mm. Here it is a green and pleasant land, quite unlike the bleak and arid, stereotyped image of the high plateau. The mean annual temperature here is about 10°C, the summers warm and humid. As the land can sustain arable agriculture and livestock, the people of this region are settled farmers rather than nomadic herders.

The Qinghai-Tibet Plateau is known as the 'roof of the world', but 'penthouse' might be a better description. Not that there is anything luxurious about most of this enormous upland plateau. Even in midsummer snow flurries are not unusual and the ground is covered with hoar frost in the early morning. Some areas resemble arctic tundra, with the ground frozen to a depth of 100 m or more. Even so, the sun is very strong, creating 20°C swings in shade temperature during the day, and the high ultra-violet levels can tan skin to leather. On the northern slopes of the Himalayas, and on most of the Qinghai-Tibet Plateau itself, rain is rare, averaging less than 200 mm in north and central Tibet, and this, together with the thin soils, can support only the sparsest of plant cover. Mountain steppe is the dominant vegetation type, mainly grasses, such as feather grass (*Stipa purpurea*), and plants such as alpine kobresia (*Kobresia pygmaea*). Above the mountain meadowland, shrubby cinquefoil (*Dasyphora fruticosa*) predominates in a zone of low-growing vegetation, an adaptation to the constant wind and sub-zero temperatures.

Despite these harsh conditions, there are some places which seem to offer water and the promise of succour for both Man and beast. Thousands of lakes dot the Qinghai-Tibet Plateau (Tibet alone boasts more than 1500) covering a total of 30 974 km², more than a third of China's total lake surface. In this land of low rainfall, melting snow from the numerous high peaks is the major source of their water. But, more often than not, what appears to be an oasis of fresh water turns out to be a sea of brine. Rather than eventually flowing to the sea, many lakes in this region drain by evaporation, gradually concentrating the dissolved salts that were originally garnered from the mountain and swept into the lakes. China claims the greatest number of salt-lakes in the world, many rich in soda, gypsum, boron and other minerals deposited as the stagnant water evaporates. The largest saltwater lake in China is Qinghai, whose waters (with a salinity of 12.49 g per litre) are more than four times more salty than the sea. Despite its high salt content Qinghai Lake is home to a number of endemic fish species, among them the *hua yu*, a scaleless fish famed in local cuisine for its delicate flavour. Many seabird species seem to regard the salt-lake as an acceptable alternative to their ocean home, and cormorants (*Phalacrocorax carbo*) and black-headed gulls (*Larus icthyaetus*) nest here in large numbers. Bar-headed geese (*Anser indicus*) also migrate to the lake for breeding during spring and summer, flying over the Himalayas from their wintering grounds in India.

Human beings may find the Qinghai-Tibet Plateau's climate inhospitable but many animal species thrive in this cold, arid world. Several species of lizard are adapted to the cold of the region; they are viviparous, holding their eggs safe and warm inside their bodies and giving birth to live young. A few snake species can also be found and the pit viper (*Agkistrodon strauchii*) is endemic to this super-upland.

Surprisingly, although quite sparse, the grass on this highland steppe is very nutritious, containing high levels of protein and fat. Such vegetation can support many kinds of herbivores, everything from rabbit-sized marmots (*Ochotona thibetana*) and the endemic Tibetan woolly hare (*Lepus oiostolus*) to large herds of Tibetan gazelle (*Procapra picticau-data*), wild ass (*Equus kiang*), Tibetan antelope (*Pantholops hodgsoni*) and, the king of the super-upland's herbivores, the yak (*Bos mutus*). A close relative of the now-extinct aurochs of Europe, the yak is a massive beast, weighing as much as a tonne and with a temper to match its size, quite in contrast to the more tractable domesticated variety. On the higher levels ibex (*Capra ibex*), blue sheep (*Pseudois nayaur*) and the huge-horned argali or Marco Polo's sheep (*Ovis ammon*) eke out a living, moving to lower pasturelands only in winter. Bird life includes the Tibetan snow cock (*Tetraogallus tibetanus*), black-necked crane (*Grus nigricollis*), lammergeier (*Gypaetus barbatus*) and alpine chough (*Pyrrhocorax graculus*).

In a world in which so much wild game exists, it is surprising that more carnivores have not evolved to survive in the harsh environment and so exploit this rich source of food. Only the ubiquitous wolf (*Lupus canis*) and that most beautiful of all the big cats, the snow leopard (*Panthera uncia*), earn their living on this high plateau. Both wolf and snow leopard have become increasingly rare in recent years, due primarily to hunting for the fur trade but also

because of a catastrophic decline in the number of all wildlife (including their major prey species) on the Qinghai-Tibet Plateau.

Less than 30 years ago, the area round A'nyemaqen was known as 'China's Serengeti', a reference to the huge numbers of antelope, gazelle, ass and yak that grazed there. 'China's Great Plains' may be a more useful analogy today, for history is repeating itself. About 150 years ago, the great herds of ungulates on North America's Great Plains were devastated by the advancing wave of European pioneers. So too today; indiscriminate hunting and an influx of settlers from China proper has brought about a drastic reduction in the numbers of all herbivore species living on the Qinghai-Tibet Plateau. Over the past ten years or so new varieties of high altitude grains have been developed. This has encouraged traditional nomadic peoples to take up a more settled farming existence, further exacerbating the situation and making the parallels with nineteenth-century North America even more pronounced. Such permanent farming means an end to the sharing of resources between herders and wildlife; the natural world is completely excluded from the area of settlement. In addition, the increased population that settled farming can sustain means an increased demand for meat over and above what domesticated livestock can provide. Wild ungulates are the 'logical' means of supplying this demand, further tightening the screw on the indigenous herbivore population. At present, it is only in the far west of the region that the wild creatures are found in anything like their former numbers, and even here there are signs that increasing human settlement is beginning to encroach upon the last strongholds of Tibet's unique fauna.

Pika burrows after a fall of fresh snow, Qaidam Basin.

SNOW LEOPARD

SNOW LEOPARDS (*Panthera uncia*), ALSO KNOWN AS 'OUNCES', HAVE A THICK, greyish white coat dotted with black rosettes. Adults are about 2 m long, including the well-furred 76 cm (2½ ft) long tail, and weigh no more than 45 kg. The paws are enormous and not only help the animal to grip its prey, which can be three times its size, but also assist it in walking in deep snow and in keeping its balance after leaping.

RANGE Once sparsely but widely distributed in the mountainous terrain of Central Asia, from the Tian Mountains in the north, south across the Qinghai-Tibet Plateau to Nepal, and west along the Himalayas to the Hindu Kush in Afghanistan, the snow leopard's range has shrunk over the years in all countries but the largest portion still remains in China. Here, the snow leopard is found in Xinjiang Uygur and Xizang (Tibet) Autonomous Regions and in Sichuan, Qinghai and Gansu Provinces.

HABITAT The snow leopard is found between 3000 and 6000 m in high alpine meadows and rocky ground above the treeline. It prefers broken terrain with cliffs but also travels across fairly gentle terrain, especially if there are ridges that provide travel routes and shrubs and rock outcrops that provide cover.

BEHAVIOUR Solitary by nature, snow leopards rest up and raise their cubs in rock cavities which they use for several years. These lairs are often lined with thick mats of moulted fur. Male and female meet briefly to mate but the rest of the time they hunt on their own, the only exceptions being females with young. Males start to seek out mates in early spring – February to March, depending on the latitude and altitude. They court and mate for 2–3 days and have been observed to cooperate in hunting. Gestation averages 96–105 days and litters of two to three cubs are born, mainly between April and June. The cubs open their eyes about 8–9 days after birth and their eyesight quickly matures to that of an adult by 3 months of age, when they start to hunt. The juveniles leave their mother at 1 year old.

A study carried out in the Langu Valley in west Nepal on five radio-collared snow leopards revealed them to be active at dawn and dusk, resting during the day. Their home ranges varied widely between 12 and 39 km². The animals did not appear to be territorial as their ranges overlapped almost completely and there was no evidence of them patrolling home-range boundaries. But the animals themselves kept their distance (separated by 1.9–2.3 km), confirming their solitary nature. The five individuals shared a favourite area, or 'core area', within the overlapping home ranges where they spent about half their time. The core area represented less than 25 per cent of the total home-range area. It was located at the confluence of a number of streams where topography and vegetation cover were favourable and prey were abundant. The snow leopards marked the core area much more

Opposite: Hunting for its pelt, and declining prey numbers, have made the snow leopard (*Panthera uncia*) the rarest of all leopards.

Overleaf: Snow leopards come together briefly in early spring for courtship and mating.

frequently than other parts of their home ranges, which suggests that scat sites are important in communicating information between individuals and in helping to space them. The average daily travelling distance was small for a large carnivore, about 1 km, but this was probably a reflection of the leopards' preference for hunting in one favourite spot.

The snow leopard's diet features a high proportion of blue sheep or bharal (*Pseudois nayaur*). In Taxkorgan Reserve in Xinjiang (see below, Schaller *et al.*, 1987), blue sheep comprised 60 per cent of the leopard's diet (29 per cent was Himalayan marmot (*Marmota himalayana*). In Schaller *et al.*'s (1987) Qinghai/Gansu study area, blue sheep comprised 30–40 per cent of the snow leopard's summer diet and marmot made up the rest. Schaller and his team worked out that, in the 6 months of summer, a snow leopard kills about 35 marmots and 5–6 blue sheep. Other ungulates are not preyed on, probably because they are now so scarce. Blue sheep are the most numerous of the ungulates (1–5 per km^2 in Qinghai, with some herds containing more than 50 animals) but they too are declining and the snow leopard has to compete for them with wolves. Livestock was a minor food in summer but this almost certainly increases in winter, especially as marmots hibernate and are no longer available to the leopard.

A snow leopard showing threat behaviour.

STATUS The snow leopard is very threatened in all parts of its range. Y. Liao from Xining's People's Park carried out a study in 1985 of snow leopard distribution in Qinghai Province based on capture records of animals for zoos. The study revealed that there were snow leopards in 20 counties. The populations were substantially larger in four counties: Qilian, Tianjun, Dulan and Zadoi.

In the summer of 1985 and 1986, George Schaller and a group of Chinese co-workers assessed the status and distribution of large ungulates and carnivores in the western half of Taxkorgan Reserve in China's Xinjiang Uygur Autonomous Region (Schaller *et al.*, 1987). The survey was part of a 4-year project to assess China's high-altitude wildlife resources. Taxkorgan Reserve, located in mountainous terrain about half of which is over 4500 m, was established in 1984 primarily to protect these animal groups. The surveyors made counts of snow leopard by combining information on their scrapes, spoor and droppings with information on habitat availability and prey density. They estimated that there were only about 50–75 snow leopards in the reserve. Interviews with local inhabitants confirmed a very sparse distribution, mainly in broken terrain with cliffs, the habitat that ibex (*Capra ibex*) and blue sheep also prefer. Snow leopards were very scarce in certain areas, e.g. the mountains rimming the Chalachigu and Upper Taxkorgan Valleys, and this was a reflection of the scarcity of prey. In the Mariang area, where prey was more plentiful, snow leopards were more common.

Blue sheep and other species of ungulate have been severely reduced in numbers by the Kirghiz and Tajik locals for their meat, which is consumed locally as well as exported. This reduction in the prey population has had a very negative effect on snow leopard numbers, as has shooting them to preserve livestock. From scat analysis, livestock appeared to comprise a mere 5 per cent of the snow leopard's diet but the scat sample obtained in livestock areas by Schaller and his co-workers was not taken during winter when, according to herdsmen here and elsewhere in the leopard's range, most damage is done. Moreover, people often find and remove a carcass before it is eaten, which means that there are more livestock killed than eaten by the snow leopard. A more realistic figure of livestock predation by the region's four predators (snow leopard, wolf, red fox and brown bear) was derived from data collected by the Mariang commune and confirmed by interviews, namely, an annual loss of 616 sheep and goats and 58 large animals (yak, camel, cattle, horse, donkey). This works out as 3.3 sheep and goats and 0.3 large animals per family per year, or 7.6 per cent of the sheep and goats and 1.7 per cent of the large animals in the total livestock population.

The reserve's ungulates have to compete with domestic livestock for grazing pastures and, in some areas, these pastures are being reduced to desert as a result of people cutting trees for making roofs and for fuel. The occasional juniper tree is all that remains of a species that was once common below 3500 m. Where there are no trees, the people serve their fuel requirements by digging up low-growing shrubs, such as *Artemesia* and *Ephedra*.

For 7 months in the summers of 1984 to 1987, Schaller and another team of Chinese scientists extended the survey of snow leopard in China to the Provinces of Qinghai and

Gansu (Schaller, Junrang & Mingjiang, 1987). The census was a continuation of the project undertaken to assess China' high-altitude wildlife resources. In Gansu, they found snow leopards only in a few places along the western and southern edges of the Province, namely the Qilian Mountains and the Daie Mountains. The Gansu populations, with perhaps some in Sichuan Province, represent the eastern limit of snow leopards in China. Their status in Qinghai was better. The cats inhabited all the major mountain ranges in Qinghai and a number of small massifs, occurring in over 65 000 km², or 9 per cent, of Qinghai Province. However, the biologists found that the actual range occupied by viable populations is less than this because, in some parts, herdsmen have wiped them out entirely or reduced the local population to a few stragglers; in other areas (e.g. parts of the Arjin Mountains), the mountains are so arid that wildlife is rare. They estimated that about 650 snow leopards remained in Qinghai (1 cat per 100 km²) but that human pressures were a grave threat to their survival. Even though the species was legally protected, hunters shot and trapped them for their fur and for their bones, which are used in Chinese medicine. As in Xinjiang, people were also decimating the leopard's main prey, the blue sheep or bharal. Schaller reports that, since 1958, Qinghai has exported 100 000–200 000 kg of blue-sheep meat (5000–10 000 animals) every year, much of it going to western Germany. 'Communes are assigned quotas – the Zaching commune in north Zadoi had an annual quota of 5,000 kg – and local men shoot animals of both sexes and all ages, using in some instances small-bore rifles provided by the government.' No effort is made to manage the resource on a sustained basis and, as a result, blue sheep have been eliminated from their various ranges and greatly reduced in others. The snow leopard's other major prey species, marmot, are shot for their pelts and poisoned with zinc sulphide because they are said to compete with livestock for grass. Schaller also reports that the local tribesmen use steel traps indiscriminately to catch whatever passes by – snow leopard, blue sheep, brown bear or gazelle.

CONSERVATION MEASURES The snow leopard has been protected in China since 1983 but limited funds and staff prevent enforcement and so local people continue to kill the cats and their ungulate prey with impunity. The leopards are killed mainly because they prey on livestock, even where losses are relatively small, e.g. in part of east A'nyemaquen in Qinghai where 5 households, with a total of 2350 domestic animals, had lost 12 (0.5 per cent) to both wolf and snow leopard in 1 year. Clearly, any programme to conserve the snow leopard must take account of the problem of livestock predation. It is not going to be easy as the Chinese Government is set on increasing livestock production and income from wildlife, and local human populations are still expanding. Schaller suggests that Qinghai should establish reserves for large mammals, contiguous with those in Xinjiang Uygur Autonomous Region and Gansu Province, in which human activities should be controlled. Education through religion, suggests Schaller, could be helpful in convincing the mainly Buddhist herdsmen to curtail their hunting.

WILD ASS

THE KIANG OR WILD ASS (*Equus kiang*) IS THE ONLY MEMBER OF THE EQUIDAE TO inhabit the Qinghai-Tibet Plateau. Asses differ from horses by lacking 'chestnuts' on the hind limbs and long hairs on the tail. They have thinner manes but rather longer ears. They retain the 'wolf-tooth' – a peg-like first premolar – into adult life and have a simpler enamel pattern on the teeth. Many details of skull anatomy are also different (Groves, 1974).

The wild ass is the largest of all the world's asses, standing (at 1.42 m at the shoulder) as tall as Przewalski's horse (*E. przewalski*) and weighing up to 400 kg (adult male weight; females weigh 250–300 kg). The massive head has a broad 'roman' nose and is carried on a thick neck. The short body has long legs, with broad hooves, and a tufted tail. The ass's lips are thick and its palate horny, an adaptation to the sharp siliceous plants on which it feeds. The coat is russet-red and the white of the underside extends onto the legs, the side of the neck and the throat. The muzzle is also white with white rings around the eyes and

Above: The wild ass (*Equus kiang*), forerunner of the domesticated donkey.

Overleaf: A wary herd of wild ass on the high steppe of Qinghai Province.

inside the ears. There are three subspecies: *E. k. kiang*, which has a distinctive winter coat of deep auburn; *E. k. holdereri*, the largest of the wild asses; and *E. k. polyodon*, the smallest, only 1.10–1.15 m high.

RANGE There are three main distribution areas, corresponding to the three subspecies. *E. k. kiang* ranges across the south-western part of the Qinghai-Tibet plateau, around Gnarikhorsum and across the frontier into Ladakh. Recent work by Chinese researchers suggests that the species may range as far as the mountains of the northern edge of Tibet bordering Xinjiang Uygur Autonomous Region (Gao & Gu, 1989). *E. k. holdereri* has the most extensive range, estimated at 1 500 000 km², from the Qilian Mountains of Qinghai in the north, to the easternmost extension of the super-upland on the borders of Gansu and Sichuan Provinces and south as far as the Brahmaputra River (Yarlung Zangbo Jiang). Just to the south of the Brahmaputra, but effectively isolated from its relative by this mighty river, lies the range of the third subspecies, *E. k. polyodon*. From this southernmost area of the plateau they are said to occasionally traverse the Himalayan passes and enter Bhutan and Sikkim.

HABITAT The wild ass lives on high steppe land, from 4900 to 5700 m. The land is composed of bare, broken mountain ridges and swampy valleys with the occasional salt-lake interspersed with broad plains. There are no trees and the vegetation is composed mainly of xerophyllous plants and grasses such as purple-flowered needle grass (*Stipa purpurea*), Krylov's fescue (*Festuca kryloviana*) and Moorcroft's sedge (*Carex moorcroftii*), the last-named being endemic to the Qinghai-Tibet Plateau.

BEHAVIOUR The wild ass is a herd animal, as are all Equidae. Herd size varies enormously, from five animals up to 400 or more. In earlier times, herds of over 1000 wild asses were regularly seen. Except for the mating season, these herds are composed entirely of adult females, their juvenile offspring and their young-of-the-year. Each herd has as leader an old mare, experienced and wise in the ways of the plateau. From the age of 6 years or so, the young stallions leave the herd and live alone for most of the year, ranging and feeding at a higher altitude than the female-plus-young herds. They return to the vicinity of the herd towards the end of July, but it is not for another 2–3 weeks that the mating season gets into high gear. The male chases vigorously after the females, cutting out individual animals time and again and herding them all together into his own 'harem'. Competition between males is fierce and fights are frequent. The rut lasts for about a month, by which time all the eligible females have been covered and are carrying young.

Gestation takes almost a full 12 months, the young being born in late July/early August. With such a tiny infant to care for, females are effectively out of commission during the following rut, so that each female can give birth only once every 2 years. Development of the foal is swift; by November the youngsters are close to half-grown and well able to keep up with the herd. By the time the next rut comes round they are often fully independent.

Those foals, still tied to their mother's apron strings, are rudely separated by eager stallions. Apart from this mother–infant bond, wild asses are rather aloof creatures, with the minimum of social interaction. While Przewalski's horses spend a lot of time in mutual grooming behaviours, the wild ass seems to prefer to do its own toilet, nibbling or scratching the skin wherever it can reach.

A herd of wild asses is almost impossible to approach. They have excellent eyesight and can spot a man at over a mile on the flat, bare plateau lands. When the wind is favourable, they can scent even a hidden man at more than 400 m. In 1986, we sent two experienced cameramen, Andrew Anderson and Ben Osborne, into Qinghai Province to film the animals there. Although they managed to film many species, including birds of prey and blue sheep, the only shots we saw of kiang were 'long shots' of herds in the far distance, and even these were taken with telephoto lenses! Apart from Man, the kiang's only enemy is said to be wolf (*Lupus canis*), and perhaps Tibetan brown bear (*Ursus arctos*). The wolf employs its favourite strategy when hunting wild asses, following the herd patiently to identify the young or sick, which they then attempt to cut out and isolate from the rest of the herd before closing in for the kill.

Many of the grasses and other plants in the wild ass's habitat are tough and leathery, and most produce spicules of silica in an attempt to deter grazing. But the lips and mouth of the wild ass are specially adapted to this rough fare, and they feed happily on plants that would lacerate the mouth of many other herbivores, their favourite being the aptly named speargrass (*Potentilla gelida*).

STATUS Chinese estimates of wild ass populations on the Qinghai-Tibet Plateau are in excess of 200 000 individuals of all subspecies (pers. comm.). In some areas, the wild ass is still considered common (for example, an aerial survey of the Arjin Shan Nature Reserve in 1984 found 41 262 wild asses to be present in the reserve, a density of almost one ass per square kilometre (Gao & Gu, 1989). However, the picture is by no means as rosy in other areas. To Tibetans at the turn of this century, the wild ass was a sacred animal and its killing was forbidden. Europeans and Chinese had no such taboos and have hunted the animals for sport and food. But there are more subtle ways of killing an animal than simply shooting it. With increasing population and the influx of many immigrants from China proper, the living space available to the wild ass, as for most other wild ungulates, has declined appreciably in recent years. While the wild ass is not yet severely endangered, if present trends continue, the future can only be considered bleak.

CONSERVATION MEASURES Although Chinese law gives the wild ass the same Class 1 protected status as, for example, the giant panda or white-lipped deer, there are no specific projects and proposals to aid this species. It does, however, gain a measure of protection in reserves set up to conserve other species or groups of species. In particular, the setting up of the Chang Tang Nature Reserve (see p. 15), to protect an entire intact ecosystem, should do much to ensure the survival of this species.

WHITE-LIPPED DEER

THE WEST FIRST LEARNED OF THE WHITE-LIPPED DEER (*Cervus albirostris*), KNOWN by Tibetans as *shou*, from the Russian explorer Przewalski. It was later 'rediscovered' and described by W. G. Thorold, hence its other common name, Thorold's deer. Adult males weigh over 200 kg and are 1.3 m tall at the shoulder. The species is distinguished by pure white on the nose, chin, lips and throat. It has a short head and a short, wide muzzle and the hoofs are wide, like those of an oxen, with pseudo-claws that are especially well developed and long. The coat, mostly brown lightening to cream on the belly, lacks a woolly underfur but is dense and twice as long in winter as in summer. There is a 'saddle' on the withers, formed by the hairs growing in the opposite direction, and females have a short tuft between the ears. The antlers slant backwards, unlike those of red deer (*Cervus elaphas*), which point upward. The flattened beams have five to seven points and there is a large space between the first and second points.

RANGE The home of the white-lipped deer is the Qinghai-Tibet Plateau, between 92.5° and 120° E and 29.5° to 38.7° N, the Qihai Mountains in north-eastern Qinghai and the mountains of western Gansu and western Sichuan.

The pale pelage, or hair, on nose and lower jaw characterize the rare white-lipped deer (*Cervus albirostris*).

HABITAT These deer live between 3500 m and 5000 m in rhododendron scrub, alpine grasslands and coniferous forests. In Qinghai and western Gansu, Schaller, Junrang and Mingjiang (1988) found them high up on grass-covered ridges, the crests of which are used by snow leopards as travel routes. White-lipped deer share their habitat with Tibetan gazelle (*Procapra picticaudata*), Asiatic wild ass (*Equus kiang*), blue sheep (*Pseudois nayaur*) and domestic livestock, such as horses, yak, sheep and goats.

BEHAVIOUR Over the past 10 years the white-lipped deer has been studied by Chinese, Japanese and Polish biologists. It is a social animal, moving around its grazing pastures in loose, mixed-sex, mixed-age groups of about 25 animals for most of the year. But, with the onset of the rut in September, the herds separate into harems of about ten does, each group headed by a stag. In 1986, biologists from the North-West Institute of Endangered Animals in Xining observed eight harems in Yushu and Goluo Prefectures in Qinghai Province and Garze Prefecture in Sichuan Province. The rut is a period of great activity for mature stags. They fight with one another for the privilege of holding a harem and this involves much roaring, head-down threat postures and aggressive head-on clashes and locking of antlers. The larger, stronger stags are usually the winners but, because they are totally occupied with winning, defending and mating with their females, they have little time to eat and quickly lose condition over the 2-week period. Does are also more excitable during the rut, licking the males and wallowing with them in pools of mud. Those stags without harems keep their distance but bide their time for when the harem-holder has lost so much condition and status that they can make a successful play for the harem. Their position is second-best nevertheless because most of the does will have been impregnated by the time they come on the scene.

Deer herds tend to be unstable and individuals frequently join and leave the herd. The only lasting association is between a mother and her fawn and sometimes also a yearling. However, Miura *et al.* (1989) found the deer around Gyaring Lake in Qinghai to be very cohesive, probably because of the pressure of constant hunting by locals. Once the rut is over, harems again coalesce into larger groups of variable size, with some males tending to be loners or form small groups. Schaller *et al.* observed herds of between 18 and 92 animals in Qinghai while Miura and his team studied one herd containing 25 deer around Gyaring Lake. This herd consisted of 14 adult females, 7 fawns and juvenile females and 4 juvenile males between 1 and 4 years of age. It had a mobile home range of 35 km², moving between feeding areas in a cyclical fashion with a home range of about 35 km². Gestation lasts about 8 months (230–250 days), the does giving birth between late May and late June. Only one fawn is dropped per female and, as the deer mate only once a year, a female can produce a maximum of only one fawn a year. As soon as the fawn is born, the female licks it clean and half an hour later it is able to stand. Over the next 2–3 days the female and her fawn move away from the place of birth to denser cover, usually either shrubs or tall grass. The mother always keeps within sight of her fawn and, if it is threatened, she will run in the opposite direction to that taken by the calf in an attempt to distract the predator. Fawns seem to depend on their mother's milk for extended periods. At two deer farms in China, a team of biologists observed hinds frequently suckling 1–2 year-old animals.

White-lipped deer feed mainly on grasses and sedges but many other plant species are also eaten. The team of biologists from Xining who studied wild deer in Qinghai and Sichuan found that 64 plant species were eaten but that there was a definite preference for 24 of these – mainly grasses and sedges. The white-lipped deer in this area grazed mostly in the morning and the late afternoon, the early afternoon being spent lying down or ruminating. Because stags are constantly on the look-out for predators their feeding bouts are shorter than those of does.

STATUS White-lipped deer are declining in most parts of their range, with both herd size and number of herds decreasing quite dramatically in recent years. Only scattered populations exist in areas where once there were healthy herds. The reasons are the same as those for many other ungulate species in these parts: habitat degradation and over-hunting for their horns, which are highly valued in Chinese medicine and sold in local markets. Some areas still have a fair number of deer. In South Zadoi and Shule Nanshan in Qinghai, during their survey of China's high-altitude wildlife, Schaller *et al.* estimated a maximum density of 0.3 deer per square kilometre. The deer in Shule Nanshan comprised four herds, totalling 176 animals. Miura *et al.* estimate a considerably higher density of 1 animal per square kilometre but feel that it is not very high even so. Here again, there is the problem of competition with domestic animals, especially during the winter months, causing over-grazing. Miura's survey team counted 3500 domestic animals on 1 day in the 35-km^2 home range of the deer herd that they studied. Such intense exploitation of pastures has caused severe erosion in some places.

CONSERVATION MEASURES On paper, the white-lipped deer is fully protected. Laws have been made to control hunting and there are also protected areas such as the Chang Tang Reserve in Tibet which also, at least in theory, protects other ungulate species. It is listed in the *China Red Data Book* as a Class 1 endangered species and it is also listed as a CITES-protected animal, which means that neither the animal nor any part of it can be traded. However, these restrictions are not enforced on the ground because of the shortage of funds and trained manpower. Hunts for this deer are actually advertised at a fee of US$13000 per animal and there are wealthy Westerners who are prepared to pay this price. In 1987, one German trophy-hunter was granted shooting rights for this species in Qinghai in return for a gift of two jeeps and a fee.

YAK

STANDING OVER 2 M AT THE SHOULDER AND WEIGHING IN EXCESS OF 1000 KG, THE male wild yak (*Bos mutus*) is a formidable creature. Its skull is broad and densely boned, and set off with viciously curved, 1-m-long curved horns. The female of the species is much smaller, only a third the weight of the bulls, with smaller, more irregularly shaped horns. All yak are unusual in having 14 pairs of ribs (all other oxen possess 13). The hair of the pelt grows differentially, curly on the head, long on the sides of the rump and the shoulders, and shorter but denser on the back, withers and top of the head. The tail is long and ends in a tassel. In most cases the pelt is black but golden varieties are known. Yak have rather long legs for their size, probably an adaptation for walking in the deep snow of their high-altitude environment. The pseudo-claws are well developed and help the yak in climbing steep slopes; the hooves are also enlarged, and seem to have evolved to aid movement in the swamps which cover part of its range during the short Tibetan summer.

RANGE This animal was originally found over much of the Qinghai-Tibet Plateau. Travelling in eastern Qinghai in 1889, William Rockhill (1891) described hillsides as 'literally black with yak; they could be seen by the thousands'. Even 80 years ago, the yak's distribution covered the headwaters of the Yellow River (Huang He) and Yalung River in the west of the plateau but, since then, its range has shrunk markedly and it is now restricted to remote regions of north-western Tibet (Xizang).

The thick coat of the yak (*Bos mutus*) protects it against the harsh environment of the Tibetan uplands.

HABITAT The yak inhabits the desert steppes of northern Tibet, a forbidding landscape of wide horizons and rolling plains. No trees or shrubs grow here to soften the force of the wind, which roars over the steppe lands, making the winter temperatures of −40°C feel infinitely colder. Summers are hardly any better: while the sun is above the horizon the temperature can soar up to 20°C or more but the night temperature scarcely rises above freezing.

BEHAVIOUR While old bulls may be solitary in habit (except during the breeding season), most yak are social, with young males banding together into herds of 10 or 12 animals, while groups of adult females, adolescent bulls and calves can number over 1000 individuals. Despite the herd having difficulty finding sufficient food for all its members, such large numbers provide the most effective protection for the yak's only natural enemy (apart from Man), the wolf (*Lupus canis*). Wolves normally only take young calves, or sick or wounded adults. A fully grown animal fears no four-legged predator. Ernst Schaefer (1952) reported that: 'the old bulls are grim, fierce fellows. . . . They will attack, head up, with great speed, with their tail raised like a banner which is whipped to and fro on the back.'

Yak feed on the desert-steppe plants of the plateau, which total about 30 species, among them edelweiss, needle grass (*Stipa purpurea*) and cinquefoil (*Potentilla gelida*). They tend to graze mainly on the foot-hills of the mountains, leaving the vegetation on the lower plains and the high peaks to other species. But the growing season on this roof of the world lasts a mere 3 months and, for most of the year, the yak (along with Tibetan antelope (*Pantholops hodgsoni*), gazelle (*Procapra picticaudatus*) and other herbivores) must make do with dead, desiccated vegetation. When grazing is good, the animal will stay in an area for many days, feeding, ruminating and bathing in the many creeks and lakes that dot the plateau. If food is scarce, the yak moves on. During severe blizzards it turns its rump into the wind and will stand unmoving, protected by its dense winter coat, for as long as the storm lasts.

The mating season begins in September and can last over a month. Only during this short period of the rut do yak vocalize to any degree; for the rest of the year the animal is, to all intents and purposes, silent, a fact which led the geographer and explorer Nikolai Mikhailovich Przewalski to bestow upon the yak its specific name, *mutus*. Mature bulls follow the herds of female yak at this time and fight among themselves for access to the cows. Each male endeavours to push his opponent sideways and to drive his horns into the other's flank. The fights are often bloody affairs and serious injury, sometimes even the death of one or both of the combatants, can result.

The gestation period for yak is 9 months, the females giving birth in June, just at the beginning of Tibet's brief summer. Unlike many ungulates, the calves require over 12 months care from their mothers, and the female bears young only in alternate years. The male yak reaches full maturity at 6 or 8 years of age.

The domestic yak (*B. m. grunniens*) has been the servant of human beings for at least 2000 years. Compared with its wild cousin, however, the domestic yak is a pygmy, a pale shadow of its former free state. Less than half the size of the wild yak, the domesticated variety has weaker horns, is far more vocal (it is known as the 'grunting ox') and has a much more placid disposition. The animal is absolutely indispensable to the human inhabitants of these high places, providing meat, wool, milk, cheese, and fuel (in the form of dried yak droppings). As it needs very little food and is oblivious to extremes of temperature, it is the most efficient pack animal for these high places, carrying loads of 150 kg over the steepest mountain paths with ease. Ironically, while the magnificent wild yak continues to decline, the domestic variety can be found as far west as Buchara, across all of Tibet to Sichuan, north to Mongolia and to the south into Nepal and Bhutan.

STATUS Like most of the mammals of this harsh environment, wild yaks face periodic falls in population due to natural forces, their numbers building up in good years only to be cut back by severe or unseasonal blizzards, or some other climatic disaster. They live life very much on the edge, with very little room for manoeuvre should survival pressures increase. The coming of high-powered rifles, metalled roads and ready markets for skins, meat and horn, has imposed intolerable pressure on the populations of wild yak and has swiftly led to their decline and, locally, to their extermination. At present, the animal can be found only in the bleakest areas of north-western Tibet, regions which even the nomadic hunters prefer to avoid, especially the Chang Tang, Tibetan for 'Northern Plain'. According to George Schaller (1993), who made five journeys through the Chang Tang, even there 'It is becoming exceedingly rare. Herds of 20 or 30 or even a hundred wild yak can still be seen [but] . . . in one uninhabited area of 3,200 square miles we found just 73 yaks during an intensive survey.' This reduction in numbers is due to hunting alone. Although the yak is a fully protected species in China, according to Schaller many officials (charged in theory with protecting the yak) use car and trucks to make sorties into the reserves to slaughter the animal for sport and for profit. Elsewhere, he reports finding yak heads 'littering the most remote areas'.

CONSERVATION MEASURES Several areas of the Qinghai-Tibet Plateau have been set aside for the specialized wildlife of this area, including the Altun Mountains, the Longbaotan and the Chang Tang Nature Reserves. The Chang Tang holds the distinction of being the largest true nature reserve on the planet. The Greenland National Park is larger but, as most of its area is composed of sterile ice-cap, the Chang Tang should be accorded premier position. With an area of 335 000 km^2 (960 km by 480 km at its broadest and longest points), the Chang Tang could easily accommodate the whole of the UK or Arizona State within its borders. Although there are a small number of nomads who pasture domestic stock on a seasonal basis within the reserve, their effect on the ecosystem is minimal. However, recently, small numbers of people have moved into the Chang Tang on a permanent basis, with the sole purpose of hunting the wild herbivores for their meat, pelt and horns. This is a recipe for disaster; these few reserves are the yak's only remaining safe havens. Here the yak (and all the other large herbivores of the Qinghai-Tibet Plateau) will either survive or perish.

TIBETAN ANTELOPE

OF MEDIUM SIZE, THE TIBETAN ANTELOPE (*Pantholops hodgsoni*) STANDS ABOUT 1 M high at the shoulder and is 1.3 m from head to rump, with a bushy tail of between 18 and 30 cm. The weight varies between 25 and 35 kg. The dense coat is light brown, paling to white on the belly and under the throat and chin. The male's coat changes during the rut to light grey, with black on the face and down the front of each limb. The legs are slender, ending in narrow hooves. Only the male carries extremely long, thin vertical horns and, projecting from each side of the nasal area, a golfball-sized bulge, the nasal sac; this can be inflated and seems to act as a resonator for the male's challenge calls during the rut. In both sexes the skull and face are much heavier than in other antelopes.

At the Wildlife Conservation Society in the USA, work by George Amato, cited in Schaller (1993), on the Tibetan antelope's mitochondrial DNA has put a large question mark against this species' accepted zoological classification. The Tibetan antelope may look and act like an antelope, but it may not actually belong to the antelope family at all.

Mitochondria are the cell's powerhouses. Minute organelles that produce the energy to keep the cell functioning, they are the only structure outside of the nucleus to contain DNA. In addition, as only the egg's mitochondria form part of the newly fertilized egg (the sperm's mitochondria are lost), it is possible to follow the course of evolution through the matrilineal side only. By scrutinizing the make-up of the Tibetan antelope's mitochondrial DNA and looking for similarities in sequencing with other ungulates, Amato has found that the species' closest relations are not antelopes, but goats, sheep and their kin. It may be that the antelope-like appearance of the animal is due to convergent evolution, i.e. animals in similar ecological niches evolving similar 'solutions' to the problems posed by that niche. An alternative explanation has been proposed by the zoologist George Schaller (1993). On the basis of behaviour he has observed in the Tibetan antelope, especially during mating (see p. 86), he suggests that the Tibetan antelope may be a 'living fossil'.

RANGE At one time the Tibetan antelope ranged over almost the whole of the Qinghai-Tibet Plateau. Now it is mainly restricted to the western half of the super-upland, especially on the southern steppes of the Chang Tang Nature Reserve but also in scattered populations in other remote regions.

Seemingly more at home on the Serengeti, the Tibetan antelope (*Pantholops hodgsoni*) is, in fact, well adapted to an existence at high altitude.

HABITAT The Tibetan antelope inhabits the same general environment as the kiang or wild ass (*Equus kiang*): bare steppe land with low rainfall, at an altitude of 4900–5700 m, with sparse vegetation composed of such low-lying plants as alpine cinquefoil, eidelweiss and speargrass.

BEHAVIOUR A social animal, the Tibetan antelope lives in herds for most of its life. Except during the rut, the animals aggregate in single-sex herds, the males numbering from a handful of individuals to 350 or more. The female bands can be even larger, especially during the 3-month migratory period in May or June. These female herds, comprising four separate migratory populations, travel northwards 480 km or more, following ancient, time-worn paths. Their destination is somewhere in the Kunlun Mountains where, at a site still unknown to science, they drop their young.

In August, they then make the arduous return journey southwards, this time with their 2-month-old offspring. A British officer and explorer, Captain C.G. Rawling, was one of the first people to view this mass journey across the roof of the world. He wrote: 'Almost from my feet to the north and east, as far as the eye could reach, were thousand upon thousand of doe antelope with their young . . . there could not have been less than 15 000 or 20 000 visible at one time.'

The gestation period of the Tibetan antelope is 6 months. The rut, in December, seems to occur in traditional rutting areas. At the height of the rut sometimes as many as 1000 antelopes may congregate at these sites. In common with many ungulates, the male does not defend a home range or territory but fights over possession of whatever number of females he has successfully gathered around him. Nikolai Mikhailovich Przewalski was one of the first to observe the rut and left behind the first detailed (if rather anthropomorphic) account of the behaviour. The male:

> . . . gathers a harem of ten to twenty females around him. If he sees another male at a distance, he turns his horns towards him and roars with a hollow breaking sound. This means 'Bucks will get a beating here'. Often there are hard fights with serious injuries. The harem is quite a burden to the male. As one of them – right before his eyes – walks off, he dashes after her, bleating, and tries to drive her back to the herd . . . while he tries to bring back this one female, some others run away. . . . Again bleating, he tries to catch this group – and now, to top it all, the rest of the harem scatters in all directions. This is certainly more amusing for the spectators than it is for the male. . . . He angrily paws the ground with his hooves, jerks his tail upward, shaped like a hook, and . . . challenges the opponents to which his 'unfaithful' females have fled.

Such antics have been confirmed by the naturalist George Schaller, the first Westerner to be allowed to study the large mammals of Tibet for more than 50 years. Schaller also noted that, when a female is on heat, the male 'high steps close behind her, bellows, and kicks the air with stiff forelegs. He mounts by standing bolt upright, barely touching her'. This and other male activity is typical gazelle behaviour and seems at odds with the mitochondrial DNA evidence that the species is related to sheep, goats and their relatives. Schaller has tried to reconcile the apparently opposing lines of research by proposing that the Tibetan antelope may be a relict species, a survivor of an evolutionary branch that extends back in time more than 8 million years, to the Miocene Epoch, when the true antelopes/gazelles split from the goat/sheep line.

While most of the ungulates on the super-upland seem to prefer to graze specific plant types (e.g. kiang have a taste for speargrass), Tibetan antelopes are far more catholic in their diet, feeding on a wide selection of vegetation. Like all the medium-sized plant-eaters of the Qinghai-Tibet Plateau, their main enemy (apart from humans) is the wolf-pack. Brown bears (*Ursus arctos*) and snow leopards (*Panthera uncia*) may also pose a threat to young or sick Tibetan antelopes.

STATUS Although there are no accurate estimates of Tibetan antelope numbers, there are thought to be several thousand living free on the Qinghai-Tibet Plateau. Unfortunately, as well as the ubiquitous problem of domestic herds competing for the sparse plant cover, this antelope is especially attractive to hunters because virtually every part of its body can command a high price in lowland markets. As well as shooting, trapping along well-used trails is also used to catch this species.

The meat is excellent and much in demand. Antelope wool is highly prized; smuggled from Tibet into Nepal and thence to Kashmir, it is sold as *Shah Toosh*, 'the King of Wool'. Woven into shawls and scarves, it finds a ready market in Europe and North America where items sell for enormous prices (a large shawl may fetch as much as US$8500). As if this were not enough, Chinese medicine accords great value to the horns of the male Tibetan antelope and tonnes of antelope horn have already found their way, illegally, into lowland China.

With antelope skins changing hands for US$50 a pelt, the equivalent of at least a month's wages in Lhasa (and with the hunter then free to sell both meat and horn from the same animal), it is small wonder that hunting is on the increase. George Schaller tells of five families of 40 individuals who, for the first time in the history of the Chang Tang Nature Reserve, moved permanently into the area's most heavily stocked natural area, the Aru Basin. They were there not to graze stock, but solely to hunt antelopes.

Add to these pressures the unforgiving nature of the Tibetan climate, which periodically sends blizzards so severe that whole herds can be drastically reduced, and, despite its relatively high population, the plight of the Tibetan antelope could quite easily become desperate. Such crashes also affect the herds of the local pastoralists, increasing pressure on them to find additional ways of surviving. Further hunting, of antelopes and other ungulates, is probably the easiest way out of the herder's problems.

CONSERVATION MEASURES In common with all rare Chinese species, the Tibetan antelope is strictly protected in Chinese law. At present, there are no conservation plans extant specifically for this species.

EASTERN
PLAINS
AND
YANGTZE
WETLANDS

CHINA'S CIVILIZATION GREW OUT OF THE EASTERN PLAIN. IT IS A VAST AREA covering a quarter of China, bounded by the Qin and Daie Mountains in the north, by the Xi River in the south, in the west by the Qinghai-Tibet Plateau and in the east by the Pacific Ocean. Almost 60 per cent of China's human population lives in this region. Agriculture emerged here 7000 years ago and expanded rapidly with each millennium until, today, there is very little land that has not been put to the plough and virtually no natural vegetation left. The landscape everywhere reflects the dominance by human beings: a giant allotment landscape, criss-crossed with irrigation canals and dotted by peasant houses, and by the peasants themselves working the land. Farming is still very labour-intensive with none of the mechanization of developed countries. The main crops are wheat, sorghum, sweet potatoes and rice and these are planted and harvested at least twice a year in most places. The fertility of the plain derives from a combination of abundant summer rains and vast quantities of alluvial silt carried by the great Yangtze River (Chang Jiang). The Yangtze is known to the Chinese as 'the Son of the Ocean' but it could perhaps be more aptly titled 'Mother of the Land' for, without this river, there would be no eastern plain to farm. Every year it carries some 5 million tonnes of silt and the deposition of this suspended material helps regularly to renew the soil's fertility.

The climate of this region is sub-tropical monsoon. The winters are mild (temperatures stay above freezing) and the summers are hot with July temperatures rising to 30°C. The annual rainfall varies from 100 to 2600 mm and some of it falls as winter rain, which many native plants thrive on.

The original vegetation cover of the eastern plains is subtropical evergreen broadleaf forests. With agriculture dominating the lowlands, however, the forests are now confined to the mountainous areas, mainly those which border the region in the north and west and the Wuyi Mountains in the east. These mountains are a treasure house of wildlife. They are a

Previous page: The plains of eastern China are dominated by agriculture and feed much of the Chinese population.

Above: Much of China's agriculture is still not mechanized and relies on the power of human and animal muscles.

vital part of China's natural heritage and globally important, too, as they are the only remaining havens for animals and plants found nowhere else in the world.

The only areas on the lowlands where tiny vestiges of the original vegetation survive are on village grave plots, which are sacred. It is here that birds like partridge, Himalayan blue magpie and Elliot's pheasant (*Syrmaticus ellioti*) breed. Previously a forest bird, Elliot's pheasant has adapted well to the bare open countryside, though its numbers are still kept low by hunting for the pot. Some of the smaller species also manage to co-exist with humans, including a primitive grasshopper, a giant scarab beetle and the grey froghawk (*Accipiter soloensis*). The grey froghawk has been seen nesting in the tall pagodas that line the Grand Canal, a man-made waterway that stretches from Suzhou almost as far as Beijing. It is an unusual bird of prey that will take insects and small creatures, such as the Chinese tree frog (*Hyla annectans*) which is its main prey. Chinese tree frogs breed in huge numbers in the paddy fields and are often found among the mulberry trees used in silkworm culture.

The major wetland habitat of the eastern plains is formed by the Yangtze River (Chang Jiang) and its many tributaries and freshwater lakes. The Yangtze is China's largest river and the third largest in the world. It has an enormous catchment area covering 1.8 million km^2 and its annual flow to the sea averages 100 billion m^3. The total fall of the river from source to estuary is more than 6600 m and this has made it an important generator of hydro-electric power.

The Yangtze River flows 6300 km from its icy source in the Tanggula Mountains of the Qinghai-Tibet Plateau, eastwards to the East China Sea. Starting out as the Jinsha River, it cuts through the Hengduan Mountains between Sichuan and Tibet (Xizang) and then turns abruptly north-east in Yunnan, entering Tiger Leaping Canyon. The river at this point is only tens of metres wide but bounded by snow-covered mountains so high (3000 m) that the sun reaches the river only when it is directly overhead. The Yangtze River proper starts where the Jinsha and Min Rivers meet at Yibin. Here, the river enters the Sichuan Basin, easing its pace until it reaches the Three Gorges area, named after the three most famous and spectacular limestone gorges. Then once again it becomes a churning torrent, twisting and turning through the tall, steep-sided gorges. Past Yichang, it broadens out and slows down, meandering quietly along its alluvial plain. As the river flows around each bend, it deposits silt on the inner part of the bend, where it is slower-flowing, and undercuts the bank on the outer part of the bend, where it is faster-flowing. The river gradually changes course and ox-bow lakes and fertile alluvial plains are formed. The length of the Yangtze from Yichang to Hukou in Jiangxi Province defines the middle reaches of the river. It is in the lower part of the Yangtze's middle reaches that the largest lakes of the eastern plains are found. At 3583 km^2 in area, Poyang Lake in Jiangxi Province is China's largest freshwater lake and Dongting Lake in Hunan Province is its second largest (2820 km^2). In its lower reaches, the Yangtze flows sluggishly to its delta which features many lakes and rivers linked by drainage networks. Beyond Jiangjin, the river widens to as much as 80 km across and it finally empties into the East China Sea near Shanghai, producing a landscape of mudflats, sandbanks and islands, the largest of which is Chongming Island.

Wetland plants consist of aquatic plants and water-loving bankside plants. Aquatic plants thrive in the lakes of the eastern plains and are submerged, floating or emergent. Common examples of submerged plants are: bamboo-leaved pondweed (*Potamogeton malaianus*) and litter naiad (*Najas minor*). Free-floating plants include common duckweed (*Lemna minor*) and common ducksmeat (*Spirodela polyrhiza*). Among those that are anchored to the bottom but have floating leaves are floating heart (*Nymphoides cristatum*) and the large golden waterlily (*Euryale ferox*), which has long leaf stalks that extend or curl

Hoeing by hand is part of the labour-intensive system of rice farming on the eastern plain, south of the Yangtze River.

to accommodate changes in the water level. Emergent plants are firmly rooted in the mud with their leaves or upper parts standing out of the water. Examples are wild calla or water arum (*Calla palustris*) and the well-known sacred lotus (*Nelumbo nucifera*), which grows well in the shallower lakes. Lotus seeds are eaten and used in Chinese medicine and their starchy rhizomes are eaten as a vegetable or ground to a powder and used widely in the food industry.

Water-loving bankside plants consist of grasses (Gramineae), sedges (Cyperaceae), arum lilies (Araceae), bladderworts (Lentibulariaceae) and many others. A very widespread plant is the common reed (*Phragmites australis*), which monopolizes areas around lakes, ponds and river banks, forming dense reed beds between 1.5 and 4 m in height. It is used in thatching and weaving and in the paper industry. Among the herbaceous plants, which are mostly perennials, is the Chinese water chestnut (*Eleocharis tuberosa*), a popular food. Trees are represented by Chinese deciduous cypress (*Glyptostrobus pensilis*) and trabeculate alder (*Alnus trabeculosa*).

The most prolific and varied of the wetland fauna in the eastern plains are birds. Many are migrants that take advantage of the abundant food in the Yangtze catchment area, overwintering there after journeying from their northern breeding grounds. They include: cranes, e.g. the red-crowned crane (*Grus japonensis*), white-naped crane (*G. vipio*) and demoiselle crane (*Anthropoides virgo*); storks, namely, the white stork (*Ciconia ciconia*) and the black stork (*C. nigra*); swans, such as the whooper swan (*Cygnus cygnus*) and mute swan (*C. olor*); the white spoonbill (*Platalea leucorodia*); geese, represented by the swan goose (*Anser cygnoides*), bean goose (*A. fabalis*) and greylag goose (*A. anser*), among others; ducks, such as mallard (*A. platyrhynchos*), shoveler (*A. clypeata*) and mandarin (*Aix galericulata*); coots (*Fulica atra*); and grebes, such as the horned grebe (*Podiceps auritus*), the black-necked grebe (*P. nigricollis*) and the great crested grebe (*P. cristatus*).

Wetland mammals are, by comparison, much less abundant. The black finless porpoise (*Neomeris phocoenoides*) lives here, along with its better known cousin, the Yangtze dolphin (*Lipotes vexillifer*). This species is found only in China and is now very rare, limited to just a few pools and small tributaries of the Yangtze.

Among the wetland reptiles of this region are the Chinese soft-shelled turtle (*Trionyx sinensis*), a fish-eating species, and the three-lined box turtle (*Cuora trifasciata*), which feeds mainly on invertebrates. But the most famous reptile of the eastern plains is the earth dragon or Chinese alligator (*Alligator sinensis*), a species endemic to China and now very rare in the wild.

Fish are naturally abundant in the wetlands, although overfishing has drastically reduced the populations of a number of species. One such endangered species is the Chinese sturgeon (*Acipenser sinensis*), which has been over-hunted for its flesh and its eggs, which make excellent caviare. Another rare fish is the Chinese paddlefish (*Psephurus gladius*). But many other fish still thrive in these waters, especially freshwater carp, e.g. common carp (*Cyprinus carpio*), goldfish (*Carassius auratus*) and grass carp (*Ctenopharyngodon idella*), which is useful in controlling the aquatic weeds that form their staple diet.

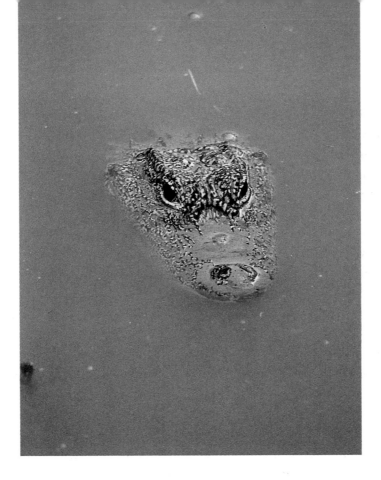

CHINESE ALLIGATOR

KNOWN AS 'EARTH DRAGON', THE CHINESE ALLIGATOR (*Alligator sinensis*) INSPIRED the fabled dragon stories that form such a central part of Chinese folklore. It was a totem of the ancient Chinese tribes living on the eastern plain but, as it became increasingly rare, strange tales were spun around it. The dragon became an object of mystery and power, so much so that war lords and emperors deified it.

The Chinese alligator is one of 21 species of extant crocodilians in the world and the only one to hibernate in winter. It is among the smallest, measuring 2 m in length and weighing under 23 kg. In typical crocodilian style, the nostrils lie on the raised tip of the nose and can be closed by folds of skin. A long nasal passage leads from the nostrils to the choanae, which open at the back of the palate. These can also be closed off by a flap of skin in the mouth, an arrangement which allows crocodilians to lurk underwater with their mouths open and still breathe – just as long as the nostrils are above the surface of the water. In fact, these animals spend a great deal of their time floating in the water, barely visible, with their body and tail angled downward, leaving only the nostrils, eyes and ears above the surface. This controlled buoyancy is achieved by a balanced distribution of air in the lungs. In common with all alligators, the large fourth tooth on each side of the lower jaw cannot be seen externally when the jaws are closed. This is because this pair of teeth fit into laterally closed pits in the upper jaw. Although the hindlegs are webbed they do not provide the

The alligator's low profile makes it easier to stalk potential prey.

power in swimming. It is the snake-like movements of its body that propel the alligator through the water, aided, when necessary, by sideways 'lashes' of the vertically flattened tail.

The Chinese alligator is strange in occupying a range along the Yangtze River (Chang Jiang) that is totally isolated from the only other alligator species (the Florida alligator) by 3125 km. How it came to be there is a question that still remains unanswered. Like its cousins, it is a very 'old' species, remaining virtually unchanged from the age of the dinosaurs. Consequently, the skin, teeth and skeleton of present-day crocodilians are similar in many way to those of the protosaurs. Judging from the numerous crocodilian fossils that archaeologists have discovered in China, many of its relatives fell by the evolutionary wayside. So far 17 genera of crocodiles have been unearthed in China, indicating great variety and numbers, and a much wider distribution than the contemporary A. sinensis.

RANGE Three thousand years ago, the Chinese alligator ranged along the lakes and marshlands of the middle and lower stretches of the Yangtze River. It extended northwards to the Yellow River (Huang He), southwards to Dongting Lake in Hunan and the land bounded by Anhui's higher peaks, westwards to Yunmeng Swamp in Hubei Province and eastwards to the Pacific Ocean. Its range today is a mere 10 per cent of this and it is now the world's rarest crocodilian. For many years, Western zoologists actually believed the species was extinct in the wild, a belief aided by the inaccessibility of Chinese scientific literature during the Mao Zedong era. But then, in 1979, during a visit to the USA, Professor Huang Chu-chien, a herpetologist from the Science Academy's Institute of Zoology in Beijing, told his amazed American colleagues that there were still Chinese alligators in the wild but numbers were very low.

The decline began as people replaced more and more wilderness with fields and villages. Many alligators were also killed because they burrowed into banks, damaging dykes and embankments. There was an extermination campaign around Nanjing in the 1980s for this reason and the persecution was repeated in other areas. Even so, 50 years ago, the Chinese alligator still flourished over a fairly wide area – in the regions of Jiujiang, Hankou, Anqing, Wuhu, Dangtu, Zhenjiang, Suzhou and Shanghai. But then there was another population crash as waterways became polluted with the chemicals and fertilizers of modern agriculture and the waste products of industry. Pressure also came from the construction of irrigation works and the further conversion of wasteland for cultivation. This involved clearing banks of reeds and grass, cover that is vital for egg development. The alligators' attacks on fish and domestic ducks and geese made it and its eggs a target for irate peasants. In some regions, people use sodium pentachlorophenate to eradicate the snails that carry blood flukes, and the alligators, which eat these snails, are exposed to secondary poisoning. A survey made between 1951 and 1956 by Zhu Chengguan (cited in Tang, 1987) recorded a much more restricted distribution than that found in the mid-1940s. The alligator could be found only near the tributaries of the Yangtze River in Anhui Province; in Zhejiang and Jiangsu Provinces it had become almost extinct. A series of surveys conducted from 1976 over a period of years revealed a further drastic shrinkage of the alligator's range and numbers.

Overleaf: The Chinese alligator (*Alligator sinensis*) is now virtually extinct in the wild.

HABITAT Chinese alligators split their time between the water and the banks of the lowland waterways along the Yangtze. They hunt and mate in the water and lay their eggs on land. In winter they hibernate in watery caves in the river bank that they excavate themselves.

BEHAVIOUR The alligator is a noisy breeder and its mating season is marked by loud, monster-like sounds that no doubt encouraged the dragon myths. At the height of the rains in mid-June roars and deep bellows can be heard for miles across the rising waters of the rice fields and fish ponds. These are the sounds of alligator males and females calling to one another. The drama reaches a climax once the male finds a mate. The pair face each other in the water, bellowing constantly, heads low on the surface and tails curved in a tight arc high up in the air. They bump snouts several times, often with a resounding clap from the impact of their bony skulls. This percussion performance is followed by the sounds of mating: deep coughs, snore-like calls and much splashing.

The females build their nests on the riverbanks about a month later. Some females guard their eggs but most are left on their own. Incubation lasts about 68 days and, 1 or 2 days prior to hatching, the young alligators 'chuck'. These calls cue the female to dig up the nest to release the young and they may also serve to coordinate activity among the young. The baby alligators break the egg open with their egg caruncle, a horny protuberance on the tip of their snout. Any that find it difficult to do so are aided by their mother, who bites through the shell. The female's help is also important in helping her charges towards the water. Huang Zhujian, one of the biologists who have studied the Chinese alligator, witnessed the death of hatchlings that had become caught up in entwined grass in the absence of the female. A mother will lure her young into the water by calling to them and will quickly take them into her mouth if they cry out in alarm. The first contact with water is usually at about 2 days of age and the yolk sac sloughs off 1–2 days after that. Young alligators grunt repeatedly while moving around and feeding, presumably to let their mothers know where they are at any time. They start off feeding on insects, worms and very small fish and gradually progress to larger prey. They lie in wait for a suitable meal, either at the surface of the water or completely submerged, often with their mouths open. The pattern of their blood circulation is such that they can remain totally submerged for up to 45 minutes.

Young alligators do not have long to experience their new water world because the cold forces them to hibernate early. By October, they have already disappeared into their hibernation dens. Some of these are simple two-roomed 'apartments', the inner room being used as a hibernaculum and to turn around in. Others are huge, complex 'mansions' with more than 20 rooms and numerous passageways, entrances, underground pools and air holes leading to the surface. The dens need to be roomy as they are occupied by several dozen animals at a time – the hatchlings and their mother, together with her young from previous years. There are other occupants as well, whose relationship to the female and her offspring is still not known.

The warmth of spring slowly draws the alligators out of their dens and, for a few days in late April, only their snout tips show at the partially submerged entrances. Then, once the air has warmed up, they slink out and bask in the sun. The frenzy of feeding that follows makes up for their 6-month fast. This is the time of year when they are most likely to be seen because their need for food overcomes their fear of humans. The prey is very varied depending on what is available: snails, mussels, shrimps, aquatic insects, fish, frogs, turtles, water birds and small mammals. Once satiated, the alligators sink back into a more sedate way of life, often returning to their dens when they get too hot. American alligators, by contrast, spend most of the summer months outside their dens. The only time the Chinese alligator moves any distance from its den is during the mating season, when the call to seek out mates galvanizes the males into action.

STATUS Today, China has fewer than 500 alligators in the wild. They are now distributed only in the border region between the three provinces of Anhui, Zhejiang and Jiangsu.

CONSERVATION MEASURES The Government of Anhui has set up nature reserves in the Province to preserve the remaining wild population. They cover five counties: Xuancheng, Langxi, Guangde, Jingxian and Nanling. In his book *Living Treasures* (1987), journalist Tang Xiyang reports that:

> Protection of the alligators is assigned to a particular lumber camp, production brigade or individual in the region where the animal is found. Those who protect the alligator are rewarded, while those who harm them are punished. If alligators ravage crops, the state compensates farmers.

The other conservation measure is captive breeding, aimed at re-introduction back into the wild. Old records suggest that the Chinese alligator was bred as long ago as 2600 BC. *The Zuozhuan* (Zuo Qiuming's commentary on the Spring and Autumn Annals, 722–484 BC)

Left: An alligator breeding pond at Xuancheng Breeding Centre, Anhui Province.

Right: The breeding programme at Xuancheng has been halted as it is over-successful: there are too many captive-bred alligators and no wild habitat into which they can be released.

mentions that, in the days of Huangdi (the Yellow Emperor) and Shun, two legendary Chinese monarchs said to have lived between 2600 and 2200 BC, there were specialists who bred 'dragons' and that this was considered a great skill. It is almost certain that this was the 'earth dragon'. The skill and fashion of breeding alligators had clearly died out by the time a modern captive breeding centre was established in 1976 in Xuangcheng County, because Associate Professor Chen Bihui had to start from scratch. There were no guidelines to consult and many problems to solve. This was graphically underlined by the fact that there were over 100 Chinese alligators in zoos across the country but none had bred. Trial and error revealed that the alligator needed space, and peace and quiet in order to mate and lay eggs. Eggs had to be incubated at precisely the right temperature and humidity and the hatchlings had to be encouraged to catch their own food and be kept warm enough for the food to digest. The care and attention paid off handsomely. In 1982, 147 eggs were hatched and 87 survived to the next year. In 1983 the output increased dramatically to 237 eggs hatched and 146 surviving through to the next year. The figures continued to improve such that, by 1992, the centre had a total of 6000 hatchlings. In 1986, zoologists from the Academy of Science's Institutes of Zoology in Beijing analysed LANDSAT satellite images of the alligator's habitat and combined this information with field surveys in order to target the best areas for re-stocking with captive-bred alligators. The results were sobering; there *were* no suitable places (Huang, Lin and Zhang, 1986). The breeding programmes at Xuangcheng and elsewhere have now been halted because there are too many captive alligators and no wild habitat in which to release them.

YANGTZE DOLPHIN

THE CHINESE CALL THIS DOLPHIN *baiji*, MEANING 'GREY-WHITE DOLPHIN'. Western scientists call it Yangtze dolphin or white-flag dolphin (*Lipotes vexillifer*). The specific name 'vexillifer', or 'flag-bearer', derives from animal collector Charles Hoy's mistranslation of *baiji*. He thought the Chinese had called it 'flag-bearer' because of the way in which the dolphin's dorsal fin breaks the surface of the water, like a white flag, when it swims. The Yangtze dolphin is China's only freshwater dolphin and a relict species belonging to the monotypic family Lipotidae. Adults are about 2.5 m long and weigh half a tonne. They are smooth-skinned, with a grey back and a white underbelly. The long slender 'beak', domed head, and low, triangular dorsal fin are very distinctive.

The Yangtze dolphin (*Lipotes vexillifer*) was once widespread along the lower reaches of the Yangtze River (Chang Jiang) but pollution and increased river traffic have reduced its numbers to less than 100.

RANGE According to Professor Zhou (1986) at Nanjing Normal University:

The range of the baiji in the Yangtse in the 1940s was similar to that at the end of the last century, i.e. ranging from the estuary of the Yangtse to Yichang, City of the Three Gorges, even up to the river by Huanglingmiao about 30 km upstream of Yichang.

By 1974, it had been pushed downstream to below Zhicheng City. Today, it is found only in the middle and lower reaches of the Yangtze River (Chang Jiang) from Zhicheng in Hubei Province to Liuhekou in Jiangsu Province. Its upstream range is no longer limited by the natural might of the Three Gorges but by human pressures, and these have reduced its number in the lower reaches as well. Illegal poaching, water pollution (from agricultural run-off and industry), a shortage of food due to overfishing, disturbance through motorized shipping, and sedimentation (from excessive erosion caused by deforestation) have combined to make survival impossible for the Yangtze dolphin. Sedimentation in Dongting Lake has become so bad that the dolphin has been forced to abandon the lake. Injuries and deaths caused by boat propellers and hook fishing add to the pressures on the species.

HABITAT The Yangtze dolphin is an inhabitant of slow-flowing rivers and lakes.

BEHAVIOUR In 1978, Nanjing Normal University and the Institute of Hydrobiology of the Chinese Academy of Sciences in Wuhan began a series of studies on the Yangtze dolphin. They looked at hunting behaviour, ecology, population density, anatomy, physiology and health management.

The birth rate of the Yangtze dolphin is low as a mature female can produce a maximum of one calf (in March to April) only every 2 years. Families consist of three or four strongly bonded members which travel and hunt together. During a hunting session, groups will execute a combination of short (10–20-second) and long (1–2-minute) dives and, when pursued by motor boat, they react with a long dive and a change of direction underwater. The dolphins use mainly echo-location to pin-point their prey but visual information is also useful. The eyes of *Lipotes* are functional, although much reduced, with a field of vision that is directed forwards and upwards.

STATUS The dolphin's rarity has prompted it to be called 'the panda of the Yangtze River'. The total population is estimated at 200–300 individuals, divided into about 42 groups in four areas along 1600 km of river. The population density within these areas is very low, about one per 4 km, compared with one per kilometre for the Indus dolphin and, similarly, one per kilometre for the Bolivian dolphin in the Ipurupuru River. Between 1973 and 1983, 33 dolphins were known to have died as a result of human pressures. This is a high mortality rate for such a small population and the rapid decline continues.

CONSERVATION MEASURES The Yangtze dolphin has been legally protected since 1975, when its capture, except with special permission, was prohibited. The legislation is now more comprehensive, operating at both central and local government levels. Two regulations issued by the State Council in Beijing – Breeding and Protecting Aquatic Resources and Strictly Protecting Precious and Rare Wildlife – both list the Yangtze dolphin among the principal species. In 1980, the Provincial Governments of Anhui and Hubei issued three notices forbidding the hunting of river dolphins. The Bureau of Agriculture, Animal Husbandry and Fishery of Anhui Province published another notice in which it stressed the importance of protecting the dolphin and other rare aquatic species. Enforcement has not been as easy, especially as far as reducing pollution and river traffic are concerned but some progress has been made on poaching, happily more through education then penalties.

However, economic development, with its attendant pollution and human disturbance, has continued apace along the Yangtze River and the dolphin is still frequently caught or accidentally injured by boat propellers. Not surprisingly, the population has continued to crash and the species is confined to only four areas. In 1979, biologists assessed the Yangtze River from Yueyang City in Hunan Province to Nanjing City in Jiangsu Province for general habitat suitability for a semi-natural dolphin reserve. They found the Tongling River in Anhui to be most suitable. A conservation centre was also set up nearby in Tongling City but this and the nature reserve were later transferred to the Jia, an old ox-bow lake off the Tongling River, 25 km south of Tongling City. The river splits the sandbank into two islands, Heyue and Tieban. The environment is very similar to the dolphin's Yangtze habitat but there are no human pressures here. The centre itself contains two pools; a holding pool containing 600 m^3 of water and a treatment pool of 150 m^3. Financed by the State Bureau of Environmental Protection, the conservation centre includes an office building, laboratory, water purification system delivering 720 m^3 of water a day and communications equipment. A fish farm has also been established at Heyue Island to supply food for the dolphins. Zhang Xian, deputy director of the conservation centre, has applied to the State Bureau of Environmental Protection for permission to remove wild dolphins from the Yangtze River and transfer them to the Tongling Reserve.

A public education campaign is helping to bring a new awareness of the dolphin's plight. This has taken many forms: awareness drives in school, published notices, the issue of dolphin postage stamps, etc. These and other measures have helped to reduce deaths due to hunting with a consequent increase in population numbers. For the first time in many years, baby dolphins were seen in 1986 in the Yangtze in Honghu County of Hubei Province. However, this hopeful sign is clouded by plans to construct a huge dam in the Yangtze's Three Gorges area which would remove more than 160 km of the dolphin's habitat.

GIANT SALAMANDER

THE LARGEST OF THE WORLD'S AMPHIBIANS, THE GIANT SALAMANDER (*Andrias davidianus*) measures up to 1.8 m from head to tail tip. Unconfirmed reports speak of lengths in excess of this for very old specimens. The skin is smooth and slimy to the touch (except on the head and throat, where small wart-like protuberances are often present) and its colour varies from a pinkish brown to almost black; mottling is often present. The head is broad and flat, with tiny eyes and a wide mouth containing small teeth. The body is robust, flattened dorso-ventrally, and carries short, weak limbs that are barely capable of moving the animal if it is taken out of water. The feet are webbed. A 'skirt' of skin runs

The giant salamander (*Andrias davidianus*) grows up to 1.8 m
in length. The males guard the spawn and look after the tadpoles
until they can fend for themselves.

along both sides of the body for its entire length. The presumed function of this skinfold is to increase the surface area for respiration across the water/skin boundary, although the primary method of oxygen exchange is via the lungs, and the giant salamander must visit the surface periodically to breathe. The tail is long and wide, flattened laterally and is the main form of propulsion when swimming. Tail length rarely equals body length and is usually around 35–45 per cent of the total length.

RANGE The genus *Andrias* comprises two species: *A. japonicus* is found in southern Japan and the Chinese species (*A. davidianus*) has a range which includes at least a dozen provinces and regions along the middle and lower reaches of the Yangtze (Chang), Yellow (Huang) and Zhujiang River Systems. The species' distribution has not yet been fully documented but it is nowhere common and its range seems to form a patchy and localized pattern. For example, in Sichuan Province, it can be found in the Daxiang Mountains, but not in the Wolong Mountains, which, with its numerous clear-water streams and water courses, appears to be ideal giant salamander habitat.

HABITAT The giant salamander inhabits clear, unpolluted streams and rivers at altitudes of 1000 m and 2500 m above sea level.

BEHAVIOUR This amphibian is totally aquatic and (unless one or two Chinese newspaper reports of tree-climbing, fruit-eating giant salamanders prove true) never leaves the water. Recent capture/recapture studies (Song, 1988) have shown that the animal is sedentary; a giant salamander caught in the October of one year can be recaptured in the same stretch of river in June the next year (9 months after initial capture). It is mainly nocturnal and excavates a depression under a rocky overhang, a lair where it lies in wait to ambush passing prey. Its diet consists of fish, shrimps, crabs and occasionally snakes and insects. When caught, the giant salamander emits a strange cry, very like a human infant in distress, accounting for its Chinese name *wa-wa yu*, meaning 'baby fish'.

The giant salamander is unusual among urodeles (tailed amphibians) in exhibiting a degree of paternal care. During courtship, the male leads the female to the nest, a depression dug in the floor of the stream, where she lays her eggs. They are immediately fertilized by the male, who then chases the female from the nest (she will apparently eat her own eggs if allowed). During the 2–2½ months it takes for the eggs to develop to the point of hatching, the male guards them continuously, driving off any potential predators. On hatching the larvae resemble partially metamorphosed newt 'tadpoles', with forelimbs, rear limb buds and external gills. The gills disappear during the third year of life, but several other larval features, e.g. teeth, are retained into adult life. At the same time that the gills atrophy, the free-swimming larva assumes the bottom-dwelling existence of the adult.

Larval development and growth has been shown to be dependent upon the temperature of the water in which the giant salamander lives and the abundance or otherwise of food.

Dark, deep pools are the preferred habitat and growth here can be almost twice as fast as in other environments. In cold water with little food the larvae can undergo a form of arrested development. Adults under the same conditions can survive for 2 or 3 years without feeding. In captivity the giant salamander has lived for more than 50 years.

STATUS There are no estimates of total population size within China, although there is a consensus that this amphibian qualifies as an endangered species. Unlike most of the animals in this book, the cause of its decline is not deforestation or human expansion. Humankind remains, however, the villain of the piece, and for two distinctly Chinese reasons. The first is the predilection, among some human members of the Middle Kingdom, for rare and exotic dishes. The flesh of the giant salamander is said to be soft and delicious and so it is in demand in some quarters as a 'rare taste' (Song, 1988). While travelling in China we have twice been offered giant salamander at small, out-of-the-way restaurants – one of which was miles from the nearest habitat of the 'baby fish' – testifying to a clandestine trade in this species, which is accorded full protection under Chinese law. We have also, inadvertently, had the opportunity of tasting 'giant salamander soup' at a banquet. The pieces of salamander flesh were most definitely not 'soft and delicious'. Strangely, our Chinese hosts were of the same opinion, but wished, just once, to taste a dish of this rare creature.

Also working against giant salamander survival is the high esteem accorded the animal in Chinese medicine. Its skin, maw and bladder are used in a number of remedies and, as the giant salamander becomes rarer, so the demand (and the price) increases. It is likely that the odd patchy distribution of the species is the result of local extinction brought about by its over-exploitation for food and medicinal purposes.

CONSERVATION MEASURES There are no known conservation plans for this species. In 1985, *China Pictorial* featured a young farmer from Zhuxi, Hubei County, named Yuan Zhichun, who had apparently begun a successful breeding programme for giant salamander. The motive in this case was profit (Yuan Zhichun was said to have supplied 2200 kg of giant salamander to nearby markets and to have earned more than 10,000 yuan profit. He was said to be breeding 1000 giant salamanders on his breeding farm, which comprised eight fish ponds of 1.5-*mu* (0.1-ha) extent. While hardly qualifying as a conservation effort, this story, if true, does show the potential for increasing the wild population through captive breeding. Unfortunately, diligent research by ourselves and our Chinese colleagues during a 1992/93 filming project in China failed to locate this breeding centre and it appears to have vanished without trace.

PÈRE DAVID'S DEER

A MEDIUM-SIZED DEER, PÈRE DAVID'S DEER (*Elaphurus davidiana*) STANDS 120 cm at the shoulder, and the stags weigh up to 200 kg. The deer are long-legged with a short compact neck. The antlers are probably the most distinctive feature of this decidedly odd-looking deer. With the main stem lying forward of the head and all the tines pointing backwards, the antlers appear to have been stuck on to the head backwards. The eyes are large, the nose almost hairless, and the dark grey-brown pelt smooth. The tail is unusually long, reaching to the heels, and the hooves are large, with an unusually wide splay, and make a clicking sound as the deer walks. The Ancient Chinese also recognized the animal's uniqueness; it was known as *ssu-pu-hsiang*, 'the four characters which do not match', a reference to the species' 'donkey' tail, horse-like gait, upturned hooves and odd-shaped horns.

The species was first brought to the attention of western zoologists in 1865 by the indefatigable missionary/naturalist Père Armand David. He had heard rumours of the fabled *ssu-pu-hsiang*, owned only by the Emperor and hidden away behind the high walls of the Nan Haizi Imperial Hunting Park, just south of Beijing. To enter the park without

Captive European Père David's deer (*Elaphurus davidiana*) have been re-introduced into China as two free-living herds.

authority was to invite execution. Even so, Père David visited Nan Haizi and, by scouting around the 70 km of wall, discovered a spot where it was being renovated. He was able to look over and was probably the first European to see the deer species that now bears his name. The Chinese authorities were eventually imposed upon to part with several animals, which were sent back to France. Most died, but four of those sent in 1870 began to breed. This small group was to be the salvation of the species (see p. 109).

RANGE Its former range is not known with any degree of certainty but the species probably extended over much of lowland eastern China and along the lower and central reaches of the Yangtze River (Chang Jiang) before the advent of the agricultural revolution. Habitat destruction, and especially over-hunting, brought about a drastic reduction in numbers. At the time of its 'discovery' (as far as Western science was concerned), the animal was to be found only in the Imperial Hunting Park at Nan Haizi.

HABITAT Père David's deer was once common on marshland and reed-covered deltas and flats close to rivers and lakes throughout the eastern plains of China.

BEHAVIOUR Nothing is known of the behaviour of this strange swamp deer in the wild, as no record of the animal in its natural habitat has come down to us. In captivity, Père David's deer form herds and feed along the margins of lakes and wetlands. Like most deer, there is a rut during which stags fight for access to females. The rut begins sometime in June and lasts for about 6 weeks. Fawns are born in March or April (the gestation period is 250–270 days).

STATUS At present, no truly wild populations exist of this species. The world population of Père David's deer numbers 1500, of which approximately 300 are in China, the remainder being spread over several countries in more than 100 collections. The population is increasing.

CONSERVATION MEASURES The four deer that made the journey to France in 1870 were far more valuable than anyone could ever have imagined. Twenty-four years later, the River Han overflowed its banks and roared down upon the Nan Haizi Imperial Hunting Park. The river was no respecter of imperial edicts. It breached the walls of the park and the last of the *ssu-pu-hsiang* made their escape, only to be pounced upon and butchered by the many peasants left starving and homeless by the deluge. Hardly any deer survived this massacre and those that did were gunned down by Western troops when the so-called Boxer Rebellion brought British and French regiments marching into Beijing to impose yet more conditions upon the hapless Emperor.

The species' last hope lay abroad. Happily the animals that had been sent to the West fared better than their relations in China. They bred well and eventually the original herd was split, with two deer being sent to England and released in the Duke of Bedford's estate at Woburn Abbey. Today, all surviving members of this species are descended from this original nucleus of just 18 animals. Thanks to the 'open door' policy which followed Deng Xiaoping's return to power, after the chaos of the rule of the 'Gang of Four', a cooperative re-introduction programme was initiated in the 1980s. In 1985, Maria Boyd and her Chinese colleagues brought 22 Père David's deer back from the Marquis of Tavistock's collection in the UK. We were fortunate enough to visit Nan Haizi Park in 1986, just a few months after these deer had been re-introduced to their new/old home, a 178-ha enclosure on the former site of the Imperial Hunting Park. Maria Boyd, who, with her Chinese colleagues, had worked so hard to make the re-introduction a success, spoke glowingly of their progress to date and plans for the future. The deer seemed to have settled in extremely well and it was a pleasure to watch these remarkable animals, walking and feeding in the shallows of the lake that forms part of the park. According to George Schaller, a second herd has already been established in captive conditions in Liaoning Province to the north of Beijing, and a third is planned for Hubei Province.

At almost the same time, a second independent project, run by the Chinese government and WWF had been working on re-introducing the species in another area of China. The site chosen was Da Feng Forest Farm, just north of the Yangtze River delta. The region is a mosaic of marsh, grassland and forestry plantation, and supports a great diversity of wildlife, as it is relatively little used by people. Thirty-nine deer, donated by British zoos (Whipsnade, Glasgow, Chester, Marwell, Knowsley and Longleat) were flown first to Shanghai and then to Da Feng, where they were released into a 120-ha enclosure. They have bred well and today the sanctuary has expanded to 1000 ha, in which over 100 animals are now living. The Chinese Government has so far spent over 1.5 million yuan in enclosing the area and building essential facilities within the park. At present, it is not known whether the herd can ever be given free-ranging status but the salt marshes on the seaward side of the reserve (unused by people) may yet prove to be suitable for such a venture. In the foreseeable future, the survival of Père David's deer would seem to be secure, at least in the small areas which humanity has been pleased to set aside for its protection.

Perhaps more than any other species, luck has played its part in the story of Père David's deer. Luck, and a chance combination of events has allowed this species to survive against all the odds. But, above all, it is the dedication and drive of the nineteenth-century priest whose name this species now bears, Père Armand David, that has been the prime force behind this species' survival.

CHINA'S LOST WORLDS: TEMPERATE MONTANE FORESTS

Among the vast panorama of crops on the eastern plains are sizeable remnants of the original forest cover. These forests, the last refuge of many rare endemic animals and plants, are all located in mountainous areas too steep for agriculture. The prominent ones are the Qin and Dabie Mountains at the northern edge of the eastern plains, the Min and Wu Mountains in Sichuan, the Wuyi Mountains of Fujian, the Hengduan Mountains of Yunnan and the Yunnan-Guizhou Plateau. These mountains stood fast when the huge glaciers scoured the land to the north during the last ice age, killing all but the hardiest species. The flora and fauna to the south were protected from the glaciers and evolved into a miscellany of indigenous life forms.

The flora of these forests is prolific and varied. There are more than 14 500 species of angiosperms and 1700 species of seed plants (nearly 60 per cent of the total found in China). Many are ancient, endemic species. Among the dominant trees are evergreen species of oak, e.g. golden-haired tan oak (*Lithocarpus chrysocomas*), evergreen chinquapins (*Casanopsis* spp.) and beeches (*Fagus* spp.). Also common are stugwoods and cinnamon from the laurel family (Lauraceae). Rare species, such as plum yew (*Cephalotaxus fortunei*), white aril yew (*Pseudotaxus chienii*) and Chinese golden larch (*Pseudolarix amabilis*) are also part of these luxuriant forests. Thriving at lower levels are numerous species of bamboo (which often form a dense understorey), wild tea and, on the ground layer, many different kinds of ferns.

This rich ecosystem abounds not only in endemic species and genera but also in endemic families, such as Bretschneideraceae, Davidiaceae, Eucommiaceae, Ginkgoaceae, Rhoipteleaceae and Tetracentraceae. Some species, e.g. the dove tree (*Davidia involucrata*), are even more unusual in being the only species and genus in their family (Davidiaceae). The dove tree is well known for its beautiful white flowers (actually bracts) that look like doves perched on the branches. We spotted two dove trees in bloom in May on Mount Emei, a sacred Buddhist mountain in Sichuan. From a distance they stood out as two splashes of white, one on either side of the valley, amid a sea of textured greens. That same autumn one of our Chinese colleagues brought us a twig heavy with fruit. They were round and hard and, we were told, they go brown when fully ripened.

Previous page: Temperate montane forest in the Qionglai Mountains, Sichuan.

Above: The gingko tree is also known as the 'duck's-foot tree' because of the shape of its leaves.

The giant of the canopy is the dawn redwood, or 'dinosaur tree' (*Metasequoia glyptostroboides*). This ancient conifer arose 100 million years ago in the Arctic and spread south to North America, Europe and Asia but it was thought to have become extinct 20 million years ago. The discovery, in 1943, of dawn redwoods in Lichuan County in Hubei Province amazed botanists. When journalist Milton Silverman visited China in 1948 to see the trees for himself he wrote: 'We found a lost world – a world that existed more than a million years ago.' Since then, dawn redwoods have been identified in other parts of Hubei Province and also in Sichuan. The tree reaches heights of 40 m and has a girth of about 2 m, but it is still less than half the size of the North American redwoods. Unlike most of the tree species in this subtropical vegetation zone, it is not an evergreen and, in fact, is the only redwood that is deciduous. The Chinese call the dawn redwood by another name, 'water larch', because it is shaped like a swamp cypress and thrives in wet conditions. In bygone days, farmers harvested the leaves and shoots to feed their cattle but it is now grown commercially for its timber in several parts of central and south-eastern China and is used as a decorative tree in towns and cities. Other conifers found only in China are catkin yew (*Amentotaxus*), Chinese swamp cypress (*Glyptostrobus*) and the Cathay silver fir (*Cathaya argyrophylla*), known as the 'giant panda of trees' because it is so rare.

One well-known endemic gymnosperm is the gingko or maidenhair tree (*Gingko biloba*). The gingko is another 'living fossil' that has survived virtually unchanged for 200 million years. Botanists in the West first heard of it in 1690 when Engelbert Kaempfer published his writings about his visit to Japan. In the Palaeozoic Era, the gingko was widely distributed in the northern hemisphere and in Australia. At a mature height of 24 m, the trees comprise part of the forest canopy and can be narrow or broadly spreading, depending on the proximity of neighbouring trees. The gingko is a deciduous species distantly related to conifers but its leaves are not at all needle-like, nor does it produce cones. The leaves are shaped like long-stemmed fans, with scalloped edges and a deep central notch, a shape which prompted one sixteenth-century Chinese writer to call it a 'duck's-foot tree'. The word 'gingko' is actually the modern name for the Japanese version of the Chinese *yin-kuo*, meaning 'silver fruit'. The gingko's male and female flowers produce yellow, plum-shaped fruit that give off an offensive smell when crushed but which contain edible seeds. Traditionally, the gingko was a prominent feature of Chinese and Japanese temple gardens; its beauty inspired the soul of the initiate and its kernels, when roasted, provided sustenance for his body. A little *maotai*, China's brand of rice liquor, was said to help the appreciation of both the gingko's beauty and its flavour.

As well as rich endemism, an interesting feature of the native flora that is found in China's eastern plains is the abundance of large genera having numerous species, particularly the trees. For example, the genus *Rhododendron* is represented by 400 species; *Quercus* and the closely related genera of *Pasania*, *Lithocarpus* and *Cyclobalanopsis* by not less than 200 species; *Litsea*, *Lindera*, *Machilus*, *Cinnamomum*, *Beilschmiedia* and other Lauraceae by about 200; *Acer* by 100; *Ficus* by a similar number; and *Magnolia* and other Magnoliaceae by 50.

The native animals of the eastern plains used to enjoy a wide distribution among the subtropical evergreen broadleaf forests of the lowlands and in the mixed coniferous/deciduous belt above. As there is little left of the lowland evergreen forests, most of the larger species are now endangered and are confined mainly to mixed forests between 3000 and 4000 m. Some species are familiar to us all, especially giant panda (*Ailurus melanoleuca*), which lives in the Qin Ling Mountains between Shaanxi, Gansu and Sichuan and in the Min Mountains of western Sichuan. The red panda (*Ailurus fulgens*), is also found in these forests but the upper limit of its altitudinal range extends above that of the giant panda. The golden monkey (*Rhinopithecus roxellanae*) is a beautiful creature with thick golden-brown fur and a striking blue face that features an up-turned nose. There is also Asiatic black bear (*Selenarctos thibetanus*), Asiatic wild dog (*Cuon alpinus*), clouded leopard (*Neofelis nebulosa*), golden cat (*Felis temminckii*) and masked palm civet (*Paguma larvata*). Ungulates include the heavily built takin (*Budorcas taxicolor*), the dainty tufted deer (*Elaphodus cephalophus*) and musk deer (*Moschus moschiferus*), which is of great economic importance to the Chinese. Bamboo rats (*Rhizomys* spp.) live in huge underground burrows from which they seldom emerge. They pull down whole bamboo plants by the root and eat everything – leaf and stem as well as root.

The pheasant family arose in this region of China and so pheasants are well represented here. Temminck's tragopan (*Tragopan temminckii*) is found mainly in the mountainous forests of south-western China between about 2200 and 3500 m. The endemic Chinese tragopan (*T. caboti*) lives in the subtropical forest of the south-east (around the Wuyi Mountains) at an altitude of about 1000 to 1400 m. Brown-eared pheasants (*Crossoptilon mantchuricum*) are restricted to the mountains of Shaanxi and Hubei Provinces. Other pheasants of the eastern plains region include silver pheasant (*Lophura nycthemera*), koklass pheasant (*Pucrasia macrolopha*), Lady Amherst's pheasant (*Chrysolophus amherstiae*), the golden pheasant (*C. pictus*) and common pheasants (*Phasianus colchicus*), which were widely introduced into Europe and North America as wild and domestic birds.

The Qin Mountains support an especially rich variety of plant and animal life. This mountain range bisects China east to west and is the watershed for the Yellow River (Huang He) to the north and the Yangtze River (Chang Jiang) to the south. The Dabie Mountains further east continue the division almost to the Pacific coast. These two mountain chains are the dividing line between the rice-growing south and the wheat-growing north. The marked diversity of the mountains stems from their latitude. They are in the transitional zone between the subtropical evergreen broadleaf forest of the eastern plains and the warm temperate deciduous forest to the north and so have an admixture of wildlife from both areas. They also mark the boundary between two major zoogeographic areas: the Palearctic to the north and the Oriental to the south. Subtropical animals such as tree frogs (Rhizomyinae), crested porcupines (Hystricidae), jacanas (Jacanidae) and flowerpeckers (Dicaeidae) predominate on the south side of the mountains, while warm temperate species, such as jumping mice (Zapodidae), Holarctic tree creepers (Certhiidae), and sand grouse (Pteroclididae), dominate the northern flanks.

Opposite: The endangered Temminck's tragopan (*Tragopan temminckii*), one of China's many species of pheasant, lives in the undergrowth of Sichuan's montane bamboo forest.

Overleaf: Golden cat (*Felis temminckii*) can range in colour from gold to the marbled appearance here. It is one of several small cat species that inhabit the forests of Sichuan's mountains.

At 3000 m Shennongjia is the highest peak in the Qin mountain range, and is known as the 'Treasure House of Plants'. It sustains a profusion of plants, many of them important in Chinese herbal medicine and many of them rare and difficult to find in other parts of the country. A local legend tells that Shen Nong, meaning 'Divine Husbandman', was an emperor *c.* 2800 BC who was an expert on traditional medicine. In order to find a herb for one of his patients, he climbed a mountain and had to erect a scaffolding to get at the plant which grew on sheer cliffs. The mountain was therefore called Shennongjia, 'Shen Nong's scaffold'. Shennongjia's soils are very varied and the topography equally so, with sharp outcrops and deep gullies juxtaposed against the more gentle inclines of mountain valleys. Rainfall is plentiful and, because the slopes are steep, a traveller can experience all four seasons in a day's climb: midsummer at the foot, spring in the lower valleys, autumn halfway up and winter among the peaks.

The vegetation occurs in fairly distinct altitudinal bands, the bottom level consisting of the subtropical evergreen broadleaf forests that once covered the eastern plains. Within this band is the herbaceous layer that is especially well endowed with rare and valuable plants. China's earliest recorded inventory of medicines, Shen Nong's *Canon of Herbs*, lists 365 medicinal herbs, many of which are found on Shennongjia, and the *Huainanzi* (written in the Han Dynasty, 206 BC–AD 220 by, it is believed, Liu An, Prince of Huainan) tells us that Shen Nong 'tasted hundreds of [the] herbs himself . . . some days as many as seventy poisonous herbs'. Among them is golden hairpin (*jinchai*), which made the ideal diplomatic gift for emperors and heads of state and was taken by famous Chinese opera singers to protect their voices. It is a difficult herb to collect because it grows on sheer rock faces and, it is claimed, within the sound of rippling mountain streams. Some herbs have charming local names such as 'a pearl on the head' (because in autumn the plant bears a fruit the size of a large pearl) and 'a bowl of water on the head'. Other important herbs include fritillary (*Fritillaria cirrhosa*),

Opposite: Women of the Tang minority group searching for 'grass worm', a fungus-infected caterpillar highly valued in traditional Chinese medicine, in the western Qionglai Mountains.

Above: Medicine-seller displaying traditional Chinese medicines of both plant and animal origin. These are highly valued and demand often outstrips supply.

ginseng (*Panax ginseng*), Japanese ginseng (*P. pseudoginseng*), anemone (*Anemone hupe-hensis*), Chinese angelica (*Aralia chinensis*), savior grass (*Potentilla freyniana*), deerhorn (*Cornu cerri pantotrichum*), and pearl fragrance (*Valeriana officinalis*). Many are collected on Shennongjia to this day (the equivalent of about 250 tonnes of crude drugs every year) but at least as many again are now cultivated. Wild and cultivated drug species provide two-thirds of the Shennongjia region's annual income (2 million yuan).

Higher up on Shennongjia, these broadleaf forests become mixed with conifers until, eventually, they give way entirely to conifers. In his travels across China (1987), Beijing journalist Tang Xiyang visited Shennongjia and described his view of the highest vegetation level looking down from Unnamed Peak at 3104 m:

> What we saw was entirely different from the complex vegetation growing further below. Here, three kinds of plant greeted the eye: tract upon tract of arrow bamboo danced in the wind like a solid ocean reaching far to the horizon, and on this ocean red clouds drifted. No! They were alpine rhododendrons bursting with joy. Against this light-red and pale green background, clusters of firs stood tall and straight. Dressed in green, they unfurled their bannerlike crowns along the rocks in the mountain breeze.

Opposite: The mountains of China's 'lost worlds' are drained by many white-water rivers such as this one.

Above: There are over 400 species of rhododendron in the mountains of south-west China.

GIANT PANDA

A LARGE BEAR-LIKE CREATURE, THE GIANT PANDA (*Ailurus melanoleuca*) STANDS
1 m tall at the shoulder and weighs in the region of 100 kg. It has a distinctive black and
white pelage, the majority of the fur being white, with black ears and eye patches, a band
of black fur extending across the shoulders and down the arms, and black 'trousers' on the
hind limbs.

Although Chinese writings from the Western Chou Dynasty (more than 3000 years ago)
contain references to a 'white bear', the giant panda was unknown in the West until 1869.
On 23 March of that year, after months of searching for the semi-mythical beast, the
intrepid missionary/naturalist Père Armand David was shown the freshly killed body of the
legendary white bear. One week later, he was given an adult, also dead. He wrote to his
friend Alphonse Milne-Edwards:

Ursus melanoleucus, A.D. [Armand David] Very large according to my hunters, Ears short.
Tail very short. Hair fairly short; beneath the four feet very hairy. . . . I have just received
a young bear of this kind and I have seen the mutilated skins of adult specimens. The colours
are always the same and equally distributed. I have not seen this species, which is easily
the prettiest kind of animal I know, in the museums of Europe. Is it possible that it is new
to science?

Opposite: Even in winter, bamboo provides the giant panda
(*Ailurus melanoleuca*) with a supply of nourishment.

Above: Giant pandas have strong jaw and cheek muscles to
crush the tough, fibrous bamboo stems, and this is reflected in
the panda's round, 'teddy bear' face.

This last question was somewhat disingenuous. The white bear was quite clearly 'new to science'. But where exactly this species fits in the zoological scheme of things has still, after more than 120 years, to be decided. Superficially, the giant panda looks like a bear; the problem is that many details of its anatomy, e.g. tooth structure and the pseudo-thumb derived from an elongated wristbone, link the giant panda to the red panda, which is almost certainly allied to the racoon family (Procyonidae) not the bear family (Ursidae). Some specialists believe the giant panda to be an aberrant bear, others that it is a racoon that has evolved a bear-like shape because of its diet, unique among the Carnivora (see below). At present, the majority of researchers incline to the former view, largely because of the evidence of biochemical tests, such as chromosome number and banding, gel electrophoresis and DNA hybridization. The ancient Chinese were similarly perplexed; their word for panda, *Xiong-mao*, means 'bear-cat'.

RANGE During the Middle Pleistocene Epoch (between 1500 million and 100 000 years ago) the giant panda was widespread throughout China, being absent only from the Eastern Plains. Altogether, signs of giant panda occupation have been discovered at 48 sites in 14 provinces, from Beijing to southern Yunnan, and from Shanghai in the east to Sichuan in the west. Fossil giant pandas have also been discovered in Vietnam and Burma. Today, the position is far different. The giant panda can be found in only six small mountainous regions: in the Qin Ling Mountains of Shaanxi Province; in the Min Mountains straddling the border of Gansu and Sichuan Province; and in the Qionglai, Liang, Da Xiangling and Xiao Xiangling Mountains of Sichuan Province.

HABITAT The giant panda lives in montane forest at altitudes of between about 2000 m and 3000 m. In times past the giant panda undoubtedly lived lower down; indeed it may even be that the species would prefer lowland forests. But unfortunately, today, it is agriculture, not altitude, that sets a lower limit on the panda's range. Terraced fields extend up many mountainsides to a height of 2000 m, effectively confining the panda to the heights.

At the lowest level, the panda's present domain consists of mixed forest of evergreens, such as hemlock spruces (*Isuga*) and spruces (*Picea*) and broadleafed species such as beech (*Betula*), maple (*Acer*) and cherry (*Prunus*). It also ranges higher, into predominantly coniferous forests of firs such as *Abies faxoniana*, interspersed with a few hardy deciduous varieties such as birch (*Betula utilis*). Rhododendron is present in a bewildering array of species, but the understorey in both conifer and mixed forests is dominated by wide swathes of bamboo: arrow bamboo (*Sinarundinaria fangiana*) at higher altitude and umbrella bamboo (*Fargesia robusta*) lower down. Observation is especially difficult among the dense stands of bamboo and it has taken many hours of patient study, by both Western and Chinese scientists, to unravel the secrets of the giant panda's life cycle.

BEHAVIOUR A very anomalous creature, the giant panda, although classed as a meat-eater, eats plants, and one plant in particular, the bamboo. Why this has happened has

Previous page: Adult pandas climb only in the mating season, but juveniles occasionally climb for fun.

Right: The giant panda has widely overlapping home ranges, each about 5 km² in size.

perplexed zoologists since the creature's discovery but its seems that, long ago, the panda 'decided' to put all its evolutionary eggs in one basket and to bank on the fact that, by eating bamboo, it would escape competition for food with most other species and have an abundant, all-year-round source of food. Over millions of years the panda's skull and jaws have adapted to bamboo-eating: the 'cute' moon-face so beloved by human beings owes its shape to enormous masseter (cheek) muscles providing tremendous power for the crushing jaws. The jaws themselves are massive, with enormous, flat pre-molar and molar teeth that can grind the hard fibrous stems of bamboo with ease. The giant panda's human-like habit of holding food in its hands is another example of adaptation to feeding on bamboo. One of the creature's wristbones, the sesamoid, has become especially enlarged so that it protrudes from the animal's palm to form a sixth digit, a 'pseudo-thumb', which, like our own thumbs, is opposable and allows the giant panda to handle bamboo stems with masterful dexterity.

Unfortunately, the rest of the giant panda's anatomy has not yet caught up with its hands and head. This is especially true of the panda's gut. What the animal really needs is a plant-eater's alimentary canal: tortuously long and containing cellulose-digesting bacteria so that the vegetation can be broken down efficiently and the maximum energy extracted. What it has is the gut of a meat-eater – barely six times its own body length (a sheep's gut, by comparison, is some 25 times the length of its body) and hopelessly inefficient when it comes to extracting energy and nutrients from bamboo. It has been calculated that a 90-kg panda must consume close on 20 kg of bamboo each day to derive the energy and nutrients it needs. In spring, when pandas feed almost exclusively on succulent bamboo shoots, the amount of vegetable matter consumed can rocket to 45 kg per day, about half the animal's total body weight. To survive, a giant panda must keep its stomach and intestine crammed full of bamboo, and the only way to do this is to eat day and night. This is just what the animal does; eating for on average 8 hours during the day, taking a 4-hour nap, then eating 8 hours of the night away before taking a second 4-hour sleep, after which it wakes to begin a new day of bamboo-eating. Despite this, the giant panda still lives on a knife-edge, barely able to extract sufficient nourishment to survive on its chosen diet.

This 'failure' impacts on just about every aspect of the giant panda's life. The animal is solitary, living in a home range of 3.9–6.4 km², although females tend to keep to a core area of 30–40 ha, while males range more widely. But the animal is not territorial. This is probably a consequence of the abundance of bamboo and the panda's extremely limited energy reserves. The bamboo 'resource' is simply spread out over too large an area to allow it to be defended efficiently. Females do not share any part of their home range with other females, but a male's home range overlaps not only with those of other resident males but also with those of several females. The only time that the sexes come together is during the brief breeding season, sometime in late April or early May.

As a solitary animal, the giant panda has very little chance of direct interpersonal communication. A panda's face has a very small repertoire of expressions, probably reflecting the paucity of direct social interaction and the difficulty in communicating visually in the dense bamboo thickets. Vocalizations take the place of both expressions

Opposite: Giant pandas eat about half their body weight in bamboo each day.

and body posturing in communicating emotional states. The panda has about 11 different vocalizations, although many can blend imperceptibly one into another, depending on the level of excitement, fear, etc. There is a great variation in calls, everything from a moan through a dog-like bark to a bleat that can sound for all the world like a sheep or goat.

Aside from signalling emotional states vocally, most other communication is achieved by depositing scent. Odour has a great advantage over both visual and auditory communication – it persists over a far longer time period. It can also convey information long after the depositor has left the immediate area, a major consideration in so solitary a species. Scent-marking normally takes place at specific sites, usually prominent rocks in the forest or the trunks of large trees. These sites are concentrated along mountain ridges, passes, and other areas where, because of ease of travel, panda 'through-traffic' is likely to be high.

Droppings and urine probably leave a simple 'I'm here' message but scent, a dark, musty substance produced by glands around the anus and genitals, carries far more subtle details. With our limited sense of smell, we can only guess at the amount of information these posts contain but they must convey details of the identity and age of the depositor, its sex, how recently it has visited the scent site and, perhaps most important, its readiness to mate.

Bringing male and female together at the right time during the breeding season is absolutely critical to the panda's reproductive success. The female's receptive period is extremely brief: she is on heat for 12–25 days each year, with a peak fertility, when she must be inseminated by the male, of only 2–7 days. Both sexes undergo definite behavioural changes during peak heat. They actively search out other members of their species, a far cry from the retiring anti-social *persona* they assume for the rest of the year. Scent-marking

Above: During periods of bamboo flowering and die-back, giant pandas may migrate long distances to find areas of green, unflowered bamboo.

Opposite: Courtship is the only time when adult male and female giant pandas come together for extended periods.

increases in intensity and calling becomes more frequent. (George Schaller, one of the pioneers of giant panda research, heard around 88 per cent of all calls between March and May.)

Because of the extensive overlap between home ranges, when a male does come face to face with a female he may also find other males just as eager as himself. Fights between males for possession of a female are common and they can be bloody affairs. In this situation, for male pandas, size *is* everything; the larger panda almost invariably scares off his rivals (in one case the victor chased an opponent over a 6-m precipice). Mating, like courtship, is noisy. As the male mounts the female there is a succession of barks, yips and squeals but, at the moment of intromission, both male and female normally give voice to a series of goat-like bleats that, to the human listener, verge on the comical. The male mounts the female frequently while they are together but, at the end of the peak heat period, the pair (and rival hangers-on) lose their sociable natures and revert to a solitary existence.

The panda embryo undergoes a variable period of 'suspended animation' (delayed implantation) within its mother and birth can be at any time between 3 and 5½ months

Males have to time their advances accurately because of the female's short, 2–3-day period of heat.

following conception. The fertilized egg develops into a ball of cells (the blastocyst) no larger than a pinhead, which then free-floats in the fluid of the mother's womb instead of (as in most mammals) becoming implanted immediately into the wall of the womb. Delayed implantation is found in a number of other mammal species (e.g. bears) and it seems to have evolved as an attempt by the animal to produce young only when external conditions mean that there is a good chance that they will survive. If food is in short supply during this period, the blastocyst fails to become implanted and the female is spared the huge investment of energy that pregnancy normally entails. If, however, food is plentiful, a surge of the hormone progesterone thickens the womb and the embryo is implanted and develops normally to term.

Birth can take place in a variety of nest-sites: a bamboo thicket, a cave or, more usually, a hollow at the base of an old, overmature tree. The nest is lined with bamboo or the branches of birch, fir or rhododendron. As birth approaches, the female loses interest in food and sits with her back to the tree hollow, effectively blocking the entrance and preventing the entry of predators. The young are tiny, toothless, blind and naked. Indeed, weighing just over one-thousandth of the mother's weight, the giant panda holds the record for the smallest infant-to-mother weight ratio in the placental mammals. Once born, the infant rarely leaves its mother's arms for the first 3 weeks of life. It feeds frequently, suckling up to 12 times a day for about 30 minutes each time. Between times, the female grooms and licks her baby and there is some evidence that the female's saliva contains a potent antibiotic which helps fend off many infections (hand-raised infants succumb far more often to such diseases).

At about 4–6 weeks of age, the female moves her infant out of the den. The youngster is well furred by now and the distinctive black and white markings are prominent. The mother now resumes her normal activity pattern, carrying the baby in her mouth as she travels around her home range and secreting the infant in a dense stand of bamboo while she feeds. This is probably the most perilous time in a panda's life. While adult animals are normally free of predators – leopard (*Panthera pardus*) or Asiatic wild dog (*Cuon alpinus*) may, on rare occasions, prey on an adult panda – a 1–2-month-old infant is fair game for any carnivore, from a yellow-throated marten (*Martes flavigula*) upwards. Provided the youngster survives this stage, its chances of survival increase markedly. It is fully weaned at about 8 or 9 months of age and will finally leave the protection of its mother at 18 months.

STATUS The giant panda numbers no more than 1000 individuals. Just under half the population live a precarious life in forests outside the formal reserves. The remainder enjoy a more protected existence in reserves. Yet, even here, the same three major problems continue to threaten the giant panda's survival: habitat loss, poaching, and inbreeding.

First among these is habitat loss from both agriculture and logging. Giant panda areas are almost invariably remote and difficult to police. In many cases, the areas have been settled for generations, the people farming the valley bottoms and (because poverty and lack of medical facilities kept numbers low), living in some form of equilibrium with the natural world. Recent changes which have immeasurably bettered the life of the people have destroyed this balance, with disastrous consequences for the wildlife. Increased health care has meant lower infant mortality and an expanding population. In those areas inhabited by minority groups (who are largely exempt from, the 'one-child-one-family' policy that has been imposed on the Han majority), population has expanded at an even faster rate. The result has been that more and more of the forested hillsides have been brought under cultivation, with living space for wild creatures being steadily eroded. Increased human population also brings additional demands on the forest for firewood and for house-building. Although each family's share, each year, is minuscule compared with the size of the forest, the number of families, and the passage of time, can produce devastating consequences. Robert de Wulz and his colleagues (1988) used LANDSAT satellite images to study the changes in forest cover of giant panda areas between 1975 and 1983. The photographs showed that about half of all panda habitat had been either clear-felled or heavily disturbed in the 9 years covered by the research. Although some of the loss can be laid at the door of logging units, the major part of this degradation comes from peasant farmers 'nibbling' at the forest for firewood and timber for building.

Timber is also in short supply outside these mountain areas, especially in Chinese cities, and some degree of logging is essential to supply wood for the construction trade. Surprisingly, such forestry need not be incompatible with conservation if logging is selective and a good mix of trees and understorey, including bamboo, is left (some over-mature trees must also be spared so that the pandas can find holes at the base of these in which to nest). Sadly, many logging teams still clear-fell with no thought to the requirements of wildlife, although the practice is diminishing. The problem is compounded by both habitat protection and logging being the responsibility of a single ministry – the Chinese Ministry of Forestry – giving the members of the ministry the impossible task of being, simultaneously, both gamekeeper and poacher.

Large-scale logging also brings with it undesirable spin-offs in the form of roads and other infrastructure, without which heavy machines would quickly become bogged down. The problem is that the roads not only allow loggers in, they also open up the region to poachers and other undesirable elements.

In most cases, pandas are not the primary target of the poacher. The market in panda pelts, although highly lucrative, is thankfully small and the penalties extremely severe. Other species, such as musk deer (Moschus moschiferus), are more sought after. The male of this small secretive deer is possessed of a small 'pod' or gland, found in the groin, that secretes a thick oily substance known as 'musk'. As well as being a sovereign cure for many ailments in Chinese medicine, musk is greatly prized by perfumiers in the West as a base for their luxury products. A single pod sells for as much as 450 yuan, just over half the average yearly income for a peasant farmer and a huge temptation that many farmers simply cannot resist.

Musk deer are caught by snare, a wire noose into which the animal walks as it wanders along the many bush trails in the forest. Obviously, the more snares the greater the chance that one of them will produce a victim, and up to 40 snares can be set in a single trap-line. But snares are indiscriminate; they capture any animal unlucky enough to push a head, or limb, into the wire noose. The result is indiscriminate slaughter of other deer species, the ghoral, the golden cat, the fox, and the giant panda. Even in the premier giant panda reserve, Wolong, two pandas have been snared. A WWF ranger, Stuart Chapman, reported that a constant battle had to be waged in Wolong by the reserve authorities to destroy trap-lines that appeared each week in certain sections of the forest.

If logging and agricultural expansion affects the survival chances of pandas in specific areas, and poaching threatens individual animals, it is the problem of inbreeding, exacerbated by these activities, that may well bring about the demise of the species as a whole. As naturally lazy animals, humans always log the easiest areas first: forest margins, mountain passes, flat areas and land close to rivers for easy transport. The result is that the woodland is cut up first into a patchwork of forest and clear-felled areas, and finally into a number of forest 'islands', surrounded on all sides by agricultural land, roads and railtrack. At the last count, it was estimated that the giant pandas had been divided up into no fewer than 24 separate communities. Panda populations in each area are so small (most number under 50 animals and many are as few as ten or less) that the effect of the loss of even a single animal to poaching can be catastrophic. Most scientists agree that, as a general rule of thumb, a minimum population size of 500 animals is needed to ensure a species' long-term survival (the so-called minimum viable population or MVP). Although 1000 pandas remain in the wild, their fragmentation into such small, isolated groups means that, unless action is taken now to safeguard the species' habitat and manage the population to maximize genetic interchange, then the giant panda in the wild is almost certainly doomed to extinction in the foreseeable future.

Compounding the problem is the unusual life cycle of the giant panda's staple food. Every 60 to 120 years (the time depends upon species) all the bamboo of a single species flower simultaneously, set seed, and then die. This extraordinary behaviour, known as 'mass flowering' or 'die-back' is thought to be a specialized survival strategy. At such times bamboo seed can lie inches thick on the forest floor, a feast for mice, rats and a host of other seed predators, but it is produced in such super-abundance that they could never consume every grain, ensuring that some seed is always left to germinate and so guarantee the next generation of bamboo. But what is good for the bamboo is not necessarily good for the panda, at least nowadays. In the past, whenever a bamboo species underwent die-back, the giant panda would simply move up or down its mountain home and switch its attention to another bamboo type. Today, unfortunately, human encroachment means that often the panda has only a single bamboo species within the confines of its forest 'island'. There is no second choice to fall back on. In these conditions, die-back in the bamboo means starvation and death for the giant panda. The terrible panda mortality that occurred as a result of die-back during the 1980s should be viewed in these terms: not as a natural disaster brought about by the giant panda's reliance on a single food source, but as a human-inspired tragedy resulting from encroachment by our own species on the panda's habitat.

CONSERVATION MEASURES Efforts to save the giant panda can be divided into attempts at captive breeding (including re-introduction of captive-bred animals) and steps taken to conserve the creature's forest home. So far, there has been little in the way of systematic method in either approach. It seems astonishing but, although the red panda has had a studbook (a worldwide list of all red pandas of breeding age held in captivity) for over 14 years, the giant panda is still lacking this basic tool for scientific captive breeding. In the past few years, however, the Chinese Government has commissioned a detailed study of the best methods to save this unique species. The results, published as a 157-page document under the aegis of the Ministry of Forestry and the WWF, make clear that there are no easy options if the giant panda is to survive long term.

Captive breeding has had a long and (were it not so tragic) farcical history, especially in the West. No other animal liaison has been followed as avidly by the media and an eager public, with so few results. Only three zoos outside of China (Tokyo, Mexico and Madrid) have successfully bred giant pandas. This seems to be due primarily to the manner in which the prospective 'bride and groom' were introduced. As we have seen, in the wild, courtship is a fairly drawn-out affair, involving scent-marking, calling and, finally, physical contact. In almost all of the Western breeding attempts, the two putative lovers have been treated more like mice than pandas, being thrown together as soon as the female showed evidence of peak heat. In such circumstances, it is little wonder that breeding results have been appallingly bad.

In China the record is better; up until 1986 there have been 51 births at seven zoos. This may be due, in part, to the fact that many Chinese zoos have several giant pandas in long-term captivity at the zoo, living in close proximity to one another so that they have some chance of becoming accustomed to one another's presence, vocalizations and scent. In such circumstances it seems that familiarity breeds, not contempt, but more pandas. But even in China, all is not well; only 31 of 51 cubs born survived to adulthood. On even the most charitable estimate, infant mortality in pandas runs at an horrendous 49 per cent, almost one and a half times higher than the highest comparable figures in a survey of 29 species bred in captivity. Clearly, there is a great room for improvement in ensuring that those cubs that are born actually survive to maturity.

There are two main rationales advanced for attempting captive breeding of endangered species. First, if a captive population is self-sustaining, it will reduce or stop zoo demand for wild members of the species. Second, any 'spare capacity' can hopefully be returned to the wild and help bolster numbers in poorly populated areas, or re-populate suitable areas from which the species has been extirpated. In addition, re-introduction can help to increase genetic variability and prevent the problems associated with inbreeding.

With giant pandas, there are several barriers to achieving these laudable ends. As the National Conservation Management Plan (NCMP) points out, at present the captive population is far from being self-sustaining and effectively acts against the wild pandas, draining and not adding to the total population. It also calls for management of the entire breeding stock of pandas as a unit, a studbook, stopping the practice of sending pandas of

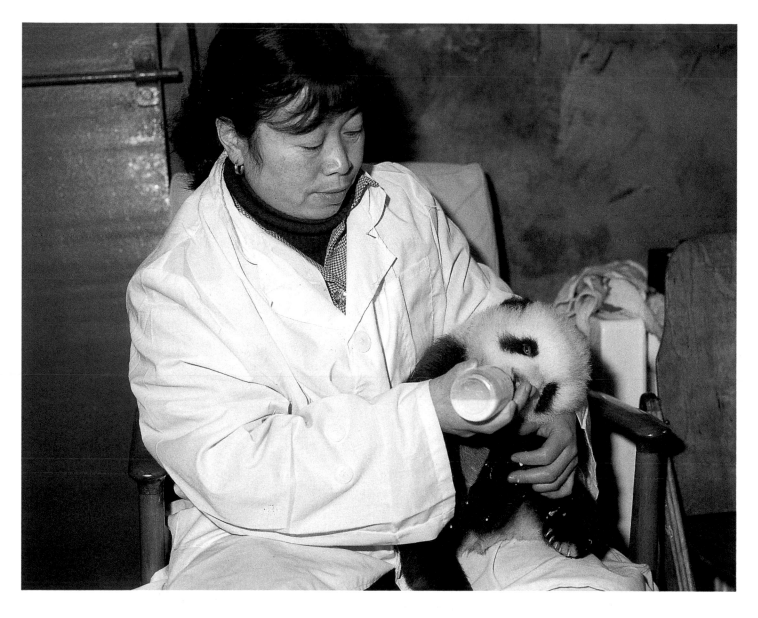

breeding age abroad (unless on specific breeding loan), and the improvement of artificial insemination techniques.

Were all these recommendations to be carried out, there is no doubt that, within a few years, captive giant pandas could supply the zoo demand for the species and produce 'excess' animals that could, in theory, be re-introduced into the wild. The big question is: can animals raised in the relatively anodyne atmosphere of a zoo survive the rigours of life in the natural world?

The answer is: probably not. At least not unless they were put through a very thorough 'survival course' to prepare them for the shock of wild conditions. The record for re-introduction does not make for optimism. Even wild-caught specimens have trouble in making the transition back to wild conditions and none have ever adapted to life in a new location. It seems that, at an early age, the animal forms a mental map of its environment (where water can be found, the location of the best bamboo stands, etc) and, once mature, finds it difficult, if not impossible, to re-adjust. With wild-caught pandas experiencing such

This 3-month-old cub was rejected by its mother, one of the females at the Wolong Giant Panda Breeding Centre, and hand-reared by staff at the centre.

problems, the chances of a captive-bred giant panda surviving without help are slim indeed. The recently published NCMP suggests several experiments that could be attempted in order to decide which method of re-introduction stands the best chance of success:

- Two-year-old captive-born pandas (fitted with radio-collars to monitor their movement) could be released into the Shiqiaohe Valley in Tangjiahe Reserve, an area with much bamboo and few resident pandas.
- Wolong Giant Panda Reserve could attempt to persuade a known, non-breeding female panda to foster an 8–10-month infant. If successful, both (radio-collared) animals should be released. With luck, the older animal will teach the younger.
- Perhaps the most imaginative scheme of all, staff at Wanglang Reserve should act as foster-parent, leading their 'panda-child' around the forest and allowing it to acquire all necessary survival skills. Once achieved, the panda would be allowed to set up its home range within the forest and, it is hoped, establish an independent existence.

In the past, habitat protection has been given scant regard compared to its more 'glamorous' cousin, captive breeding. But it is patently pointless learning how to re-introduce pandas to the wild if there is no wild left for the captive-bred animals. Panda experts now insist that habitat protection must be the first priority, and, in the NCMP, they have detailed recommendations as to how this can best be achieved. Hunting must be banned and mechanized logging phased out. Fifty per cent of pandas live outside existing reserves and their habitat should be immediately designated as new reserves (14 are planned). In many cases this would result in the land between existing reserves receiving protected status so that reserves that are presently isolated would form a single continuous panda-protected area. Within reserves, the problem of fragmented populations of pandas confined to small islands of forest should be tackled with 'green bridges'. These are specially planted corridors of trees and bamboo (0.5–1 km wide) which, once grown, would allow pandas to migrate naturally and safely between isolated groups. Artificial fallen logs should also be provided to help with natural barriers, such as rivers. Unnatural barriers, especially roads, should be regulated. In many cases, panda migration tracks could be established by the simple expedient of closing a road to traffic during the hours of darkness.

Most controversial of all is the proposal, 'demand' might be a better word, from panda experts that people living within the reserves should be removed to other areas to allow the valley bottoms to regrow and to help stop poaching and the slow attrition on woodlands. Unfortunately, the people (many of them minority groups) often do not wish to leave the valleys in which they have lived for generations. It is an extremely delicate problem but one for which an answer must be found. The experts of the NCMP are in no doubt. To save the giant panda 'there is no alternative to removing people from its last habitat, however expensive and complex that operation may prove'.

Opposite: Tibetans of the Qiang minority group in the Upper Wolong Valley, Sichuan. The Qiangs have refused to be moved to houses specially built for them further down the valley.

This policy of relocating people in order to reduce the pressures on giant panda habitat worked successfully in Tangjiahe Reserve in Sichuan.

RED PANDA

ALTHOUGH RELATED TO THE GIANT PANDA, THE RED PANDA (*Ailurus fulgens*) LOOKS more like a racoon because of its thick, banded tail, pointed ears and masked face. The foxy-looking muzzle and almost incandescent russet fur have earned it the Chinese name of 'firefox'. It is only one-twentieth the weight of the giant panda and a quarter of its height at the shoulder.

RANGE The distribution of the red panda is much more extensive than that of the giant panda. It occurs within the giant panda's range in Gansu, Shaanxi and Sichuan Provinces but it is also found in Yunnan and the south-eastern corner of Tibet. Its range also extends outside of China to northern India, Nepal, Sikkim, Bhutan and northern Burma.

HABITAT Red pandas inhabit temperate bamboo/mixed forest. This consists of conifers, mainly firs (*Abies* spp.), mixed with deciduous broadleafed species, such as birch (*Betula*

Opposite: Unlike giant pandas, red pandas (*Ailurus fulgens*) are adept at climbing trees. They are active even at night, seeking out nourishing bamboo leaves.

Above: The Chinese know the red panda as the 'firefox' from its fox-like face and bright russet fur. Its masked face also betrays its racoon ancestry.

utilis, B. albosinensis), and oak. Bamboo grows as an understorey and, where the stands are especially dense, shrubs and herbs are sparse. In Wolong Nature Reserve, there are seven species of bamboo but only two are important to giant and red panda ecology. These are arrow bamboo (*Sinarundinaria fangiana*), which grows at the higher altitudes, between 2600 and 3200 m, and umbrella bamboo (*Fargesia robusta*), which dominates the lower slopes further down, between 1600 m and 2400 m. Umbrella bamboo is quite tall, with stems averaging 2.5 m in height and just under 1 cm in diameter at the base. They grow in dense clumps, with 30–40 stems crowding into an area of 1 m². Because of this, and the way in which the long stems become tangled as they grow, moving through umbrella bamboo can be very difficult, at least for human beings. By contrast, arrow bamboo is slender, rarely thicker than 0.5 cm, and much shorter than umbrella bamboo, with an average height of 1.4 m. But what it lacks in height and girth, arrow bamboo makes up for in vigour. Stems are twice as dense as those of umbrella and its rhizomes are phenomenally active, sending out long runners that can colonize suitable habitat with surprising swiftness.

The two panda species live in harmony among the bamboo thickets. There is extensive overlap between their home ranges, even the sacrosanct core areas. The main part of the area that was studied in Wolong was shared by two to four red pandas and six to seven giant pandas, one female red panda sharing as much as 70 per cent of her home range with five of the giant pandas. And, for the most of the year, both species fed on the same species of bamboo in the same area. Yet there is little or no competition for food. This is because red pandas specialize in eating young bamboo leaves while giant pandas eat mainly stems and older leaves for most of the year. At higher altitudes, however, only the red panda exists. Its upper altitudinal limit is in fact several hundred metres higher than the giant panda's because it is more agile and can cope with the steeper slopes that giant pandas tend to avoid.

BEHAVIOUR As with the giant panda, the red panda is classified as a carnivore (meat-eater) but it feeds like a herbivore, consuming plant material almost exclusively. Around 95 per cent of this is bamboo. Without this giant grass the red panda would perish. But, unlike the giant panda, which, in the course of the year, will consume bamboo stems, leaves and shoots (gorging on the latter in spring), the red panda focuses on leaves, particularly those of the arrow bamboo. Leaves from the bottom of a bamboo stem are the ones most often taken. This is more the result of the red panda's small stature than of any dietary advantage in eating lower-growing leaves. Indeed, the topmost leaves tend to be more succulent and nutritious and, whenever it can, a red panda will climb a sapling to get at these young leaves. Red pandas select leaves with great care, meticulously nipping off one or two leaves at a time. Dead and partially dead leaves are rejected. Once selected, red pandas chew the leaves finely, which makes more of the cell content available for digestion. By its more selective feeding behaviour and thorough mastication the red panda obtains a much higher nutritional return per leaf than does its larger cousin.

Opposite: If there is a suitable 'ladder', such as a nearby sapling, the red panda will climb it to get at the protein-rich leaves at the top of the bamboo stem.

The diet of leaves is supplemented in spring with bamboo shoots and, in late summer, with the fruits of trees, particularly wild cherry (*Sorbus* spp.). There have been accounts of red pandas also eating acorns and blossoms and robbing birds' nests for eggs and chicks, as well as catching birds and small mammals. In the National Zoological Park in Washington DC, red pandas are recorded as spending a good deal of their time stalking and catching birds. Meat-eating may be linked to the greater demands on the animal during pregnancy. Certainly, among captive females, meat-eating does seem to peak when they are pregnant. As far as diet is concerned, the red panda's greater flexibility suggests that it should cope much better with changes in bamboo availability, especially during bamboo die-back.

Red panda movements have been studied with radio-telemetry in Wolong Reserve in China and in the Lantang Valley National Park in northern Nepal. They are solitary animals and very territorial. They hold exclusive, non-overlapping territories and concentrate marking around the perimeter rather than just along their trails, as giant pandas do. Males frequently patrol their borders whereas females spend most of their time in their core areas. Male territories tend to be larger than female territories, the difference being considerable in the Nepal study area (1.7–9.6 km^2 vs. 1.0–1.5 km^2) but much less so in the Wolong area (1.11 km^2 vs. 0.94 km^2) studied by Reid, Jinchu and Yan (1991). Females choose high-quality ranges, areas well supplied with food, cover and nesting sites. Males, on the other hand, are more interested in defending areas that contain as many mates as possible.

Red pandas are active for about half the day, feeding regularly during the day and night but particularly during daylight. Females tend to be more active in summer during lactation,

Like its larger cousin, the red panda has an enlarged wristbone, or pseudo-thumb, on each forepaw, which helps it to grip its bamboo food.

probably because of the need to increase their food intake. Resting is important in between feeds and red panda rest-sites are highly varied: a hollow stump, the top of a fallen log, tree stump or tuft of dead grass. Rest-site dimensions can be anything from 23 cm to 51 cm in diameter. Sometimes red pandas will dig hollows in the snow or the earth but, generally speaking, a rest-site is not modified in any way – like its giant relative, red pandas do not make nests in which to sleep. Of 18 rest-sites examined by Johnson, Schaller and Hu (1988) most were above ground level (the average height of ten sites was over 100 cm) and one of these sites was in a tree at a height of approximately 13 m. All rest-sites were surrounded by droppings, although the pandas were not averse to resting on top of a pile of faeces at five of the 18 sites studied.

There is no congregation of competing males during the mating season as there is with the giant panda because every territory-holding male already has a number of 'captive' females within his territory. He seeks out these females and mates with them as soon as they are receptive. The mating season is January to February and, for each female, the peak of oestrus, when ovulation occurs, is only 1–3 days. No one has ever observed red pandas courting and mating in the wild but studies of animals in captivity give us a good idea of what must go on. Miles Roberts and David Kessler (1979) observed male-female pairs at the National Zoological Park in Washington DC. During the mating season males follow

Above: Red pandas spend a good deal of their time sunning themselves. On cold days they conserve body heat by reducing their peripheral circulation.

Overleaf: Red pandas are much more territorial than giant pandas and keep a constant look-out for trespassers. Fallen logs and boulders provide ideal marking sites.

females at a distance and mirror their daily activities. Whenever the females marks – and she does so more frequently at this time – so, too, does the male; when she rests, he rests. In the 24 hours prior to mating, marking increases dramatically and the female becomes agitated, rubbing herself against objects and arching her tail stiffly as she moves around. The male, for his part, sniffs the female repeatedly in her ano-genital region and both of them whistle and twitter, calls which inhibit aggressive and defensive behaviour. Mating follows soon after. Mounts are few but prolonged, lasting up to 25 minutes. (In the giant panda, they are frequent and brief, lasting no longer than 2½ minutes.) The red panda male rests between copulation while continuing to clasp the female and both engage in a great deal of mutual grooming. Following in the tradition of the giant panda, the red panda male takes no further part in raising a family. His contribution to the next generation ends with the short mating period.

In spite of the big difference in body size between the two panda species, gestation lengths are very similar. Red pandas in captivity have gestation lengths of between 90 and 145 days, the shortest occurring at the lowest latitudes and the longest at the highest latitudes. This is probably because of delayed implantation (see p. 132).

Male and female red pandas come together in February or March to mate. The female's period of heat lasts for only about 3 days each year so the timing is critical.

June and July is the birth season for red pandas, 2–3 months earlier than the giant panda's birth season. Once a red panda selects her den – a rock cave or tree hollow – she lines it with leaves and tree branches, and is then ready for the trials of labour. The females of a population tend to give birth within about 2 days of one another, a sign that some sort of synchronizing mechanism is in operation. Average litter size in captivity is 1.7 young, as for the giant panda, but red pandas show more variation (one to four compared with one to three). The study in Lantang Valley National Park in Nepal reveals a lower average of 1.2, probably a more realistic figure for conditions in the wild.

Newborn red pandas are a uniform buff colour but, by 2½ months of age, just prior to their emergence from the nest, they have acquired the adult pattern and colour. Among placental mammals, the cubs of red pandas and procyonids (racoons, etc) rate as heavy in relation to the mother's weight. By contrast, the giant panda is at the top of the league table of light cub weight, while bears lie somewhere in between. Red panda cubs are blind and toothless at birth but they are much more developed and better furred than giant panda newborns. The females stay close to their young for 10 days or so, leaving them only for short periods to eat, drink and relieve themselves. A red panda mother follows the den etiquette of carnivores and eats her cub's faeces during early development, normally until the cub starts on solid food. The young depend totally on their mother's milk for the first 3–4 months and weight gain is rapid – similar to that of racoons – despite the female having a bamboo diet. The female probably manages this by mobilizing her fat reserves. Weaning begins at 4½–5 months and is complete by 6 months of age, the cub's teeth erupting in good time to cope with a bamboo diet. Nutritional independence is early enough (around September) for them to take advantage of bamboo leaves that are still tender and high in protein. It also means that they are fully weaned by the time winter sets in, so that they are no longer an energy drain on the female, who would find it very difficult to provide enough milk on an inferior winter diet.

The ties between mother and cub gradually weaken during the winter. The female becomes more intolerant of her charges and will try to avoid them, discouraging close contact with low-intensity threat displays. The apron strings are finally cut as the next breeding season approaches, when the cubs are about 8 months old. But it is another 10 months before they themselves can set up territories and breed. Until then, they are the transients of red panda society, moving through the territories of resident adults and gaining the experience and confidence that will serve them well in later life.

A female with her juvenile offspring. It is weaned but must still learn from its mother.

STATUS In times past, when the eastern plains were clothed in natural forest, red pandas ranged widely over much of this vegetation zone. But when human beings started to make an impact on the red panda's habitat with logging and agriculture its distribution shrank dramatically. This trend has been especially rapid since the middle of this century. Until recently, the red panda was found in a wide band that extended from northern India (Kashmir and Assam) through Nepal, Sikkim, Bhutan, northern Burma, southern Tibet (Xizang) and into the Chinese provinces of Yunnan and Sichuan. Since the 1940s, however, it has disappeared from much of its Himalayan range. Though data are scarce, it is now acknowledged that the red panda is extinct from eastern Kashmir, Sikkim and Assam, and that it can no longer be found over much of Nepal. Its status in northern Burma is precarious and the presence of guerilla soldiers there, together with lack of protection, hold little promise of a secure future in that region. The Bhutan populations are probably among the safest at present as much of the primary forest there still remains intact. The picture in China is unclear and a census is certainly badly needed. The red panda's greater altitudinal and geographical range would suggest a much healthier status than for the giant panda but Reid *et al.*'s field research suggests that this is very misleading. They found that the red panda is very selective as to what part of the forest it inhabits. It prefers south-facing slopes with easily accessible open areas in the forest where it can sunbathe on cold, clear days. Sunbathing is important to the red panda, which is unusual among mammals in being able to absorb radiant energy to help maintain body temperatures. At the same time, it can reduce its peripheral circulation to minimize heat loss. So essential is sunbathing to the red panda that areas in the forest with few or no sunny openings are ignored, even if they contain abundant food and nesting-sites. These constraints may well mean that the red panda is even more endangered than the giant panda, especially in view of its shrinking, fragmented habitat. Croplands presently extend as far up as 2000 m and everything below this contour is under the sway of farmers. Logging also adds to the problem. Mature firs are felled for the construction industry and the demand for this timber is such that logs are transported to far destinations in China.

CONSERVATION MEASURES In common with other rare species in China, the red panda is protected by numerous laws enacted over the past 40 years but enforcement is difficult and is much more focused on the giant panda. More often than not, the red panda in China is afforded protection because its range overlaps with that of its larger relative. Consequently, the nature reserves that help protect the giant panda should also help to protect the red panda in China.

Captive breeding is seen as a significant part of red panda conservation. In December 1993 there were 621 red pandas in zoos and other institutions around the world, 135 of them being in Chinese zoos. Many of these establishments have endeavoured over the years to breed them but, despite advances in animal husbandry, the *Red Panda Studbook* shows a sorry record of recruitment since it was first started in 1978. In the 8 years between 1978 and 1986, 217 births produced a mere ten additions to the captive population. Of newborn cubs and juveniles, 42 per cent died before reaching 6 months of age, and a further 53 per cent died in early adulthood. We witnessed these statistics at first hand in one zoo in China that is among the most successful breeders of red pandas. In July 1993, an experienced female at Chengdu Zoo gave birth to three cubs but two of them were stillborn and the other died after just a few days.

One speaker at a red panda conference in Rotterdam in 1987 looked critically at the statistics and came to a number of conclusions. The biggest culprit in cub death is stress. Females are not being given enough privacy in which to raise their offspring and, as a result, some mothers anxiously shift their young from one place to the next. This gives the mother little time to suckle them and milk production might also be affected. Food is another factor. Most zoos and wildlife parks find it impossible to supply red pandas with enough fresh bamboo to sustain their total needs. Other foods, such as fruit and vegetables, supplement their diet. Captive red pandas are very partial to this artificial menu but it seriously affects their health. Post-mortem examinations reveal severe liver damage that explains ailments such as enteritis, pneumonia, gastric disorders and circulatory problems.

Fertility in the captive red panda population has increased over the years but there is still much room for improvement. For an animal to be considered fit enough to be part of a breeding programme, it should be free of external and internal parasites. In many cases captive red pandas are infested with high levels of both and this may depress fertility. Normal hygiene and good veterinary care are all that are needed to prevent this. Fertility and, indeed, survival generally, are also affected by susceptibility to disease, and red pandas in captivity are particularly prone to infections. One speaker at the conference felt that this could be due to a naturally low level of resistance, high resistance in the wild being unnecessary if you are a fairly sparsely distributed animal.

While the captive red panda population is not in immediate danger of extinction, its future is by no means certain. Births have increased but they have not outstripped mortality, prompting the comment that 'if wild-caught individuals had not been available, the red panda would have long since disappeared from our zoos'. Zoo populations are still being bolstered by wild specimens as China continues to make red pandas freely available to zoos in Europe and the USA, despite legal protection. This may boost efforts to breed pandas in captivity, but it is not something that should be allowed to continue, given the parlous state of the red panda in the wild.

TAKIN

A VERY OLD SPECIES, THE TAKIN (*Budorcas taxicolor*) IS A RELIC OF THE PAST AND a difficult animal to classify. Some authorities assign it to its own genus (*Budorcas*) and its own tribe (Budorcatini), as it seems to stand apart from the antelopes (Antelopinae) and the Caprinae, although there may be links with both these families. Others place it into a separate family of chamois while there is yet another school of opinion that puts them in a special subfamily with the musk ox (*Ovibos moschatus*). Wu, from the Shaanxi Institute of Zoology in Xian, published a paper in 1986, attempting to clarify the takin's taxonomic affinities. He compared the body size, bones, skull, teeth and chromosomes of the Caprinae, Bovinae and Antilopinae, and he came to the conclusion that the takin was an 'ox-like sheep'. He puts the takin and the musk ox in the Ovibovinae, a grouping based on anatomy and palaeozoology. It certainly has some obvious similarities with the musk ox. They are about the same size and build – weighing approximately 300 kg and having a large head with a humped nose and a broad muzzle. The horns grow forward and curve into an angle and the legs are sturdy, the front legs being especially thickset. There are long, hard-wearing pseudo-claws on either side of the broad, round hooves. The tail is short and bushy and the coat is dense and shaggy with little difference in colour between the sexes. Run your hand along a takin's coat and it will become covered in a dark oil. This is a very efficient water-proofing agent that protects the animal from the wet, foggy air.

There are three subspecies of takin. From north to south along its distributional range coat colour darkens and body size decreases. The 'Shensi' or golden takin of Shaanxi (*B. taxicolor bedfordi*), is mainly white-yellow with very little black. Further south, the Sichuan takin (*B. t. tibetana*) is yellow, red-grey or silvery-grey with less black. The Mishmi takin (*B. t. taxicolor*) of Yunnan Province is golden yellow to brownish red, with splashes of black in many places. It is the coat of the golden takin that is believed to have inspired the Greek legend of Jason and the Golden Fleece, from a skin that had somehow found its way to Colchis. Our first sight of these impressive beasts in Tangjiahe Reserve in Sichuan was not unlike that of the American explorer-naturalist, H.S. Wallace in 1922. He wrote:

> The glasses showed them plainly – huge, golden-yellow brutes, moving easily amid the bamboo jungle on a slope so steep that they seemed to be hanging by their horns. The takin I had dreamed of, night after night, were never stranger than the animals I saw on that sunlit peak of the Tai-pai-shan. Everything about them seemed unreal – the great Roman nose, the cow-like horns and the clumsy body glistening in the sun like molten gold against the background of dull green leaves! They fitted beautifully into Greek mythology. . . .

One anatomical feature that varies with altitude is the nasal bone. In the higher-altitude subspecies this bone is in a higher position in the skull than in the lower-altitude subspecies. It is probably an adaptation to the thinner, colder air.

Opposite: The takin's (*Budorcas taxicolor*) lyre-shaped horns make formidable weapons and have been known to impale and kill hunters.

RANGE The takin originated in China and, as it extended its ranger over the millennia, it evolved into the three subspecies that we know today. The bulk of its range still lies within China in the provinces of southern Shaanxi, Sichuan and Yunnan but the Yunnan subspecies (*B. taxicolor taxicolor*) extends beyond the Chinese border into Bhutan, Burma and India.

HABITAT The takin inhabits mountains covered in dense mixed bamboo/coniferous forest in the temperate latitudes of China. Its closest living relative, the musk ox, inhabits the open, treeless tundra of the Arctic.

BEHAVIOUR Two Chinese biologists from Shaanxi Institute of Zoology and Shaanxi Foping Reserve studied takin at four sites in Shaanxi, Sichuan, Yunnan and Tibet between 1979 and 1985. Takin were found to live in groups of variable size, from family groups of about 3 animals to tribal herds of 10–30 animals. The females and their young are the core members of the family, the males often moving off on their own. One of the populations in Foping Reserve in Shaanxi consisted of 77 per cent adults and juveniles (individuals over 3 years old) and 23 per cent young. Over summer, the herds browsed on about 1200 different species of forest plant while in winter they fed on bamboo leaves, twigs and fir bark.

In the summer and autumn of 1988, and again in the autumn of 1990, Pamela Groves from the Institute of Arctic Biology at the University of Alaska, Fairbanks, carried out another study in the Qin Mountains about 150 km south of Xian, the capital of Shaanxi (Groves, 1992). She found that takin fed at all the altitudinal levels between 1600 and 2100 m that were studied. They made good use of the plant species in the area, consuming at least 84 of the 120 identified species and eating leaves, current annual growth, seeds, bark and twigs. They often trampled saplings 8–10 cm in diameter in order to reach browsable food. Large groups of 10–40 animals tended to occur only at the higher elevations, above 2100 m. The largest group was actually found just below the highest point in the study area. There was also a link between the density of vegetation and group size. At lower elevations, vegetation density was greatest and group size was small, usually less than 10 individuals, while at higher elevations, where there was sparser and more open alpine vegetation, the groups were much larger. However, to complicate matters, the takin at these greater heights tended to feed where the vegetation was densest so the formation of large groups may not have anything to do with feeding.

While filming takin in 1993 for our programme for BBC2 Television's *Natural World*, we observed three single takin in the Tangjiahe Nature Reserve. It was during a blizzard in early spring, at around 2000 m, and they were browsing on grass and herbs. Our guide informed us that in April and May they also feed on bamboo shoots, a nutritional bonanza that many other animals also take advantage of. We could not tell if they were males but they were moving up the mountain to their summer feeding grounds. When we returned in October, we encountered a large gathering herd of more than 50 animals moving down the mountain for the winter. We were told that the rut had taken place about 23 months prior

to our arrival. We kept contact with the group for several hours, watching them as they slowly moved down over the open ground and eventually faded into the wet autumn mists.

George Schaller and a team of Chinese biologists (Schaller *et al.*, 1988) studied wild takin in Tangjiahe Reserve. Takin were found between 1500 and 3000 m in herds of 10–35 animals, but some winter herds contained around 100 individuals. Adult males sometimes went against the trend in winter and, instead of joining the large herds in their downward journey, moved down on their own or in pairs. A later study carried out in Tangjiahe from July 1985 to January 1987, by a group of biologists from Nanchong Teachers' College, also found this (Ge *et al.*, 1989). They observed that most solitary males are old ones that probably no longer take part in the rut but a few of the stragglers are young and robust enough to compete in the annual contest for females. The younger solitary males never stray too far from the herds and Ge and his colleagues actually sometimes found the herds by following these 'loners'. In keeping with other studies, the researchers also found that herds contained twice as many females as males, a reflection of the fact that some males were loners. They witnessed, on a number of occasions, huge gathering herds of 127–130 animals. Gathering herds must convey some advantage to individuals and Ge and his team

The ox-like golden takin (*Budorcas taxicolor bedfordi*) is believed to have inspired the Greek legend of Jason and the Golden Fleece.

suggest that winter food may be easier to find as a large herd, or it may be that large herds help to ward off predators such as leopard (*Panthera pardus*) and Asiatic wild dog (*Cuon alpinus*).

Schaller and his colleagues found that the plants takin ate in spring and autumn were comparatively high in protein and balanced in amino acids. They also consisted of softer plant parts, with little undigestible cell wall and a good deal of easily digestible cells high in protein and starches. Winter food contained much less protein and was of much poorer quality generally, consisting of twigs and evergreen leaves from woody species.

When disturbed, takin retreat into the bamboo forest or the nearest cover. They run quickly for short distances only and have to depend on other strategies for escape from danger. One such strategy, apparently used by old (and less physically fit) males, is to flatten their bodies against the ground with necks stretched out. The takin's sense of smell is important in guiding it around its home range and in helping it to detect predators from a distance, which is particularly important as the animal cannot run at speed for long. The rut is like a sudden grand finale to the summer's quiet browsing period. It takes place in September just before the herds coalesce and move back down the mountain. For about 2 weeks the rapidly cooling mountain air is rent with the sounds of clashing horns as male competes with male for a harem of females. The winners mate and the losers bide their time until the following season. Gestation lasts about 7–8 months, with the calves being dropped in spring, their birth coinciding with the fresh growth of grass and shrubs that will boost their mothers' production of milk. They have already put on weight by the time the long climb to the summer feeding grounds begins. Takins are sexually mature by 2 years of age but do not take on the final, heavy-set adult shape until their fourth year.

STATUS Little is known of the takin's status both within and outside of China. A population estimate has been made in only one location in China, namely Tangjiahe Nature Reserve. In the reserve's 400 km², Ge and his colleagues estimated a total of 480–520 takin divided into four gathering herds on four different mountain systems.

CONSERVATION MEASURES The takin is legally protected in China and benefits from the reserves set up specifically for the giant panda.

CRESTED IBIS

A CURLEW-SIZED BIRD ABOUT 60 CM LONG, THE CRESTED IBIS (*Nipponia nippon*) has a long, thin, decurved black bill tipped with red. Around and between the eyes is bare skin, also coloured red. The neck is long and extended when in flight. The bird has rather long legs, bare from the lower half of the femur to the toes and pink in colour. The three forward-pointing toes bear small webs at their bases. There is a beautiful crest of white feathers, which hangs to the base of the neck, and the remainder of the body is covered with brilliant white plumage. In 1877, A.A. David and M.E. Oustlet gave the population of crested ibis living in China the title *Nipponia nippon* var. *sinensis* on the basis of the grey plumage this variety was said to possess, to distinguish it from the crested ibis found in Japan. However, recent work (Yasuda, 1984) has shown that all crested ibis undergo a 'greying' of the plumage during spring and summer, returning to the 'normal' white colour over autumn and winter. The colour change is believed to be associated with breeding.

RANGE During the last century, the crested ibis was widely distributed across parts of the former USSR, Korea, Japan and China. In China, it was reported from Taiwan and Hainan Island in the south, Fujian Province in the east, Gansu Province in the west, and northwards

The bird most scientists thought extinct — the crested ibis
(*Nipponia nippon*).

as far as Xingkai Lake in Heilongjiang Province, Manchuria. Its core area seems to have been in the north, around the Qin Mountains (Shaanxi Province), explaining one of its Chinese titles 'the Celestials of the Qin Ling'. In the 1930s the bird was seen in 14 provinces but its range shrank drastically thereafter and, by the 1960s, it was restricted to a single province, Shaanxi. At some time during this decade it disappeared from China. The species was considered extinct until 21 May 1981. On that day, Liu Yinzeng of the Beijing Institute of Zoology (who had spent 3 years and, in the Chinese phrase 'worn out iron shoes', in his search for the crested ibis) finally observed a single bird on the slopes of Mount Jinjiahe, in Shaanxi's Yang County. A total of seven birds were found to have survived, their final refuge a small group of old oak trees, themselves the remnants of a once-proud forest, standing in an ancient cemetery.

HABITAT Once a bird of marshland/forest, deforestation and marsh drainage for agriculture has forced the crested ibis to change its ways and forge a new way of surviving in its radically changed world. The species evolved an intimate relationship with Man, swapping marshland for rice paddy, as long as the area also provided nesting trees. Paddy fields that are irrigated over winter are especially important as food sources. In this new 'habitat' the crested ibis survived, until very recently, over a wide area. However, with the adoption of more 'advanced' farming methods, regions capable of supporting the bird have now almost totally disappeared.

BEHAVIOUR The crested ibis is a resident of Yang County. It does not migrate, although it does range more widely during winter than summer. The bird forages in the paddy fields for insects, larvae, small crustaceans and other invertebrates, using its long bill to probe the mud for prey. In January, the birds return to their nesting area (a stand of oak trees in a village burial ground) and establish territories, mate and begin nest-building. One to four eggs (average three per clutch) are laid during March or April. Male and female share incubation (which lasts 1 month) and bring food to the young chicks for about 45–50 days, after which time the young have fledged. The species has several natural enemies, including crows (*Corvus* spp.) and yellow-throated marten (*Martes flavigula*) – both of which rob the nest of eggs and nestlings – and birds of prey.

STATUS The most endangered of all China's wildlife, and one of the most at-risk of all bird species, there are about 40 wild crested ibis in Yang County, Shaanxi Province, and five captive birds at the Ibis Breeding Centre in Beijing Zoo, with a further two wild specimens in Japan, on Sado Island. These latter two birds now face certain extinction as, over the past few years, they have refused to breed and tests show that they are too old to manufacture viable sex cells. This means that even methods such as *in vitro* fertilization or fostering young birds with surrogate parents are no longer an option.

Environmental degradation appears to be the main reason for the catastrophic fall in numbers, especially deforestation and the adoption of modern agricultural practices. At its most basic, the crested ibis needs paddy fields in which to feed and tall trees in which to nest. Effluents from factories with little or no pollution control, pesticides and chemical fertilizers have made large sections of agricultural land uninhabitable for the crested ibis. In addition, new methods of rice farming have meant that irrigated winter paddy fields have ceased to exist, except in one or two more remote areas (the only areas where crested ibis can now be found). Almost all trees around villages have been cut down, the exception being those few trees on and around grave plots, reprieved by the sanctity of the ground. Hunting has also added to the stresses imposed by humans upon the species.

Ancient records show that the crested ibis once lived at much lower altitudes than at present. Pressure from a rapidly expanding and modernizing human population has undoubtedly forced the birds to move to marginal land at higher altitude. Here, pollution is lessened and the farmers still keep to the old methods of cultivation. The species will survive here, or not at all. Below is the modern, polluted world of agricultural China; above, the thick forest, devoid of feeding places. From here, the crested ibis has nowhere to go.

CONSERVATION MEASURES The only known reserve, in Yang County, Shaanxi Province, has been strictly protected by the Chinese Government. The birds are watched closely (around the clock during the breeding season) by a team of dedicated researchers, who have so far succeeded in overseeing an almost six-fold increase in crested ibis numbers.

The first captive breeding centre in China was established in 1986 at Beijing Zoo, with five crested ibis nestlings taken from the wild in Yangxian county, Shaanxi Province. The first successful breeding took place 3 years later, when two eggs were laid by a 4-year-old female bird. One was left with the female, the second incubated under a domestic fowl. Both hatched, but the ibis-reared bird died almost immediately, from wounds inflicted by either the father or mother. The fowl-reared chick survived 6 days.

In a bizarre twist of the *Jurassic Park* story, researchers in Japan have been given permission by their Government to deep-freeze the last pair of crested ibis to be found in the country. The idea is that, far in the future, it might be possible to recreate the birds from the information stored in the frozen birds' DNA. Japan's Environment Agency is sponsoring the work, which is being performed by the Japan Wildlife Research Centre. The tissue will be stored in liquid nitrogen at −196°C to await a time when the species can be re-formed from its nuclear material. The problems of hand-raising the birds, and the ever-present problem of what environment they will face in the far future, are left to future generations to resolve. Kenji Kitaura, a vet on the project, is quoted as saying: 'We have no way to save them, so we must do something.' As there is a viable population of the species not too far away, in China, it would seem more sensible to allocate the funds assigned to this 'forlorn hope' of an experiment to the successful work now going on just across the Sea of Japan. If the human race is willing to take any technological fix rather than face up to the fact that habitat protection is the *sine qua non* of species/ecosystem protection, the prospect of survival for most species on this globe will continue to be very poor indeed.

GOLDEN MONKEY

A MOUNTAIN LANGUR, THE GOLDEN MONKEY (*Rhinopithecus* (*Pygathrix*) spp.) IS endemic to China. It is a massive monkey, with large males weighing 16 kg and measuring up to 2 m from head to tail tip, although half this length is tail (the monkeys are known as 'cow-tail monkeys' on Fanjing Mountain in north-eastern Guizhou Province). The face of this monkey is the most astonishing sky-blue with an equally surprising, tiny upturned nose, accounting for its second soubriquet 'snub-nosed monkey'. In the adult, the tip of the nose forms two small follicles which grow towards the forehead. These primates are covered with long (up to 18 cm) hair, with greater or lesser amounts of gold or black, which hangs around the shoulders in a dense cape and grows longer, denser and more brightly coloured with increasing age. At one time only mandarins were allowed to use capes made from the pelt of golden monkey.

There are three distinct species of golden monkey (a related species, *R. avunculus*, is found in the rainforests of North Vietnam). Brelich's golden monkey (*R. brelichi*) is the largest. The back is covered in grey fur, the arms and head yellow, and the shoulder cape tends towards pale yellow or white.

The brown golden monkey (*R. bieti*) is slightly smaller, with the inner sides of the limbs white, a white head and black forehead, and a cape of black fur with occasional long grey hairs. The tail is also black, covered with curly hair.

The smallest of the forms, the Sichuan golden monkey (*R. roxellanae*), has a dark yellow-grey, slightly tufted tail, an overall buff to golden-orange coat and a chocolate, brownish-grey cape of fur on the back, shot through with long golden hairs.

The tiny nose and russet-gold pelt are responsible for the Sichuan golden monkey's specific name *roxellanae*. It honours a slave girl from Galicia named Roxellana. Captured by Turkish pirates, after many adventures she became the property of Suleiman the Magnificent, Sultan of the Ottoman Empire. But soon it was Suleiman who was in thrall to Roxellana, who was known as the 'Favoured Shining One' because of her huge blue eyes, delightful upturned nose and glistening red-gold tresses. Suleiman broke with a 400-year-old tradition and, in 1523, took Roxellana to wife. The type specimen of the first golden monkey to reach the West (it was sent, almost inevitably, by that arch-discoverer of Chinese wildlife, Père Armand David) was examined by Alphonse Milne-Edwards. He was so struck by the monkey's upturned nose and red-gold fur that he named the species after the slave girl.

RANGE Brelich's golden monkey is found in Guizhou Province, principally in the Fanjing Shan Natural Protected Area in the Wu Mountains, which are located in the north-eastern part of the province. The brown golden monkey is found in the north-western tip of Yunnan Province in southern China, where it probably ranges north into Tibet (Xizang),

Opposite: The golden monkey's upturned nose and blue face make it an unmistakable inhabitant of the high forest.

restricted by the Upper Yangtze River (Chang Jiang) and the Upper Mekong River (Poirier & Hu, 1983). The Sichuan golden monkey has the widest distribution of all; it is found principally in Sichuan Province but extends north and east into Gansu, Hubei and Shaanxi Provinces, where it is represented by several isolated populations. The species may also extend westwards into parts of Tibet.

HABITAT This is a strictly mountain-dwelling monkey, normally living about 1500–3400 m above sea level, and in a climate that would kill most other monkey species (snow for 6 months of the year, temperatures down to at least −10°C in winter and less than 100 frost-free days annually). The maximum vertical distribution of the golden monkey (up to 4000 m) (Li *et al.*, 1981) makes it the highest-living of all non-human primates. The species spends its time between three distinct vegetation bands:

- Coniferous forest (2800–3300 m) comprising *Abies faxoniania*, *Tsuga chinensis* and *Picea asperata*.
- Mixed coniferous and broadleaf forest (2500–2800 m), where *Picea asperata*, *Betula albo-chinensis* and *Acer davidii* are the dominant tree types.
- Deciduous broadleaf forest (2500 m and lower), where the most common trees are *Pterocarya insigna*, *Acer* sp. and *Tetracentron* sp.

The golden monkey therefore inhabits the same general 'bamboo forest' region as the giant panda, although the bamboo understorey which predominates here is visited rarely by this primate, principally during the bamboo sprouting season between March and April. Aside from this, the monkeys spend the vast majority of their time 20–30 m above ground, in the forest canopy.

BEHAVIOUR Most of the sparse research that has been done on this group of primates relates to the Sichuan golden monkey (*R. roxellanae*). The golden monkey is extremely hard to observe because of the nature of its habitat, its large home range and its ability to make off at great speed through the trees, leaving the human observer to fight his out-of-breath way over ridge after ridge of mountain at altitudes that produce breathlessness and nausea in the unacclimatized. Having ourselves spent several days in fruitless search for golden monkey (and having sent out cameramen who spent over 2 months in the forest with the reward of only the briefest glimpse of monkey), we can sympathize with the problem facing all students of this species.

The golden monkey lives in troops of varying size, from a modest 20 or 30 individuals up to an enormous 300 animals. A troop is composed of many families or 'microcolonies', each headed by a dominant male with three to five females and a varying number of young under 3 years of age (Chen *et al.*, 1983). The males fight between themselves for the possession of females and for the establishment of a dominance hierarchy, which in the long run helps to reduce the number of inter-male combats. The animals' home range is immense, between 20 km² and 50 km², and the home ranges of neighbouring troops seldom overlap. Instead, they are often delineated by a prominent geographical feature,

such as a high mountain or an open stretch of ground within the forest. The troop seems to traverse its area in a regular pattern over a period of weeks. In this the golden monkey is similar to a number of other mammal species, e.g. giant otter (*Pteronura brasiliensis*) (Laidler, 1984).

Some observers believe that the animal is exclusively vegetarian, feeding on leaves, buds, fruit and, in spring, bamboo shoots (its stomach is large and heavily sacculated, an adaptation to a diet of fruit and leaves). However, other researchers report a carnivorous aspect of the diet, with the monkeys feeding on insects and, occasionally, robbing birds' nests. Although earlier reports spoke of the troops retreating down the mountain with the onset of winter, the most recent research indicates that the animals can survive the rigours of winter with minimal changes in their foraging pattern. In this season, when heavy snow covers the land, they seem to rely heavily on *Usnea longissima*, a lichen that grows on many pine trees in golden-monkey habitat, hanging in long strands from the branches.

While foraging the monkeys give soft 'wu-wu' contact calls to maintain group cohesion. Young searching for their mothers make a characteristic 'wa-wa' vocalization (Li *et al.*, 1981). When danger threatens, the alpha male will give voice first to a 'ku-ku' call, then a crow-like 'ga-ga', after which he flees through the forest, followed by the rest of the troop, all calling simultaneously. The 'ga-ga' vocalization, when used alone, has an altogether

Golden monkeys are folivores and must spend the best part of the day feeding on young leaves.

different meaning; it is made when an animal finds a particularly rich source of food and wishes to inform the other troop members of its location.

Their daily activity pattern has two peaks: they rise at dawn and move and feed until around mid-day, when they take a 1–2-hour siesta. Following this, they continue feeding until around 5 p.m. Golden monkeys make no tree nest or other sleeping structure: they choose one or two sleep-trees each night and spend the night on the wider branches or in the crook of a limb. The animals are almost totally arboreal, although they do sometimes raid fields for peas and other foodstuffs (and have been caught in traps for their trouble). Captive animals in one zoo spent almost all their time on the high shelf in their enclosure, coming to the ground for only 2.04 per cent of any 24-hour period (Ma *et al.*, 1989).

The mating season seems to be subject to local variations. According to Happel and Cheek (1986) some golden-monkey populations breed in early spring; in others mating occurs between September and November. A detailed recent study in the Qing Mountains of Hubei Province gives the breeding season as August to October. The sexual skin of the perineal region takes on a characteristic light blue colour but the female's genital region does not swell when she comes into heat, as is normal with many other monkey species. The female solicits copulation by lying on her belly with her back straight, tail laid along the branch of a tree and looking back towards the male of her choice. The male initiates mating by chasing the female. During copulation the male's tail is held in a circle. An unusual feature of this animal's mating behaviour, at least in zoos, is that the female mounts the male almost as often as vice versa, and almost always at the instigation of the male. Such behaviour has yet to be observed in the wild and may be an artefact of the captive situation in which these particular monkeys were held.

Gestation is approximately 6 months, with the young being born around March through to May (at least in the Qing Mountains study). The infant's pelage is dark grey at birth, but soon takes on the orange-gold colour typical of the adults (Rapaport & Mellen, 1990). The infant clings tightly to the female during the first few days of life and, about the fourth day, begins to pull towards objects other than the mother. One baby raised in captivity first broke away from its mother (for a brief period) when 15 days old. *Rhinopithecus* is similar to other colobine monkeys in that sub-adults help to care for the young, a behaviour which not only helps the parents of the infant, but also gives sub-adults their first experience of child-minding, possibly increasing the survival rates of their own young when their turn comes to breed. The young males reach adulthood at about 7 years of age, the females at 4 or 5 years. During the few days following birth, the father of a captive infant initiated and maintained so-called 'vigilant' behaviour, keeping close to the female and infant and giving every indication of protecting them. Although such behaviour has not been observed in the wild, it would be surprising if it was absent. Despite its size, the golden monkey has several predators, especially when it descends to ground level to feed; among them are wolf (*Lupus canis*), Asiatic wild dog or dhole (*Cuon alpinus*), yellow-throated marten (*Martes flavigula*), falcon (the young monkeys only), golden cat (*Felis temmincki*), brown bear (*Ursus arctos*) and leopard (*Panthera pardis*).

STATUS According to a survey published in 1988 by Ma and Wang (the latest available) golden monkeys in many areas are declining in numbers (as are most other monkey species). This is disastrous news for Brelich's golden monkey and the brown golden monkey; 5 years earlier (in 1983) a report on the status of these two species described the situation as critical. Pourier and Hu (1983) estimated that the total population of each of these species was about 200 individuals, which puts each at the lower limit for long-term viability. The Sichuan golden monkey is more fortunate: its population is estimated at 3700–5700 animals. The main reasons for this decline are hunting and habitat destruction/degradation. In both Guizhou and Sichuan Provinces the population of *Rhinopithecus* is said to have increased slightly in recent years. Research presently going on in Guizhou Province indicates that the world population of Brelich's golden monkey can be uprated to a more healthy 800 individuals.

CONSERVATION MEASURES All three species of golden monkey are Class 1 protected animals and killing and capturing them are forbidden. Article 9 of the Chinese constitution states that 'the Government will protect rare flora and fauna'. In addition to such far-sighted (though admittedly vague) statements, the March 1989 Wild Animals Protection Act stipulates not less than 7 years in prison, or a fine, or both, for any person hunting any nationally protected species (a category which includes the golden monkey). As with any other country in the world, enforcement of such laws is far more difficult than their promulgation, and golden monkeys are still occasionally shot, or captured to (illicitly) supply the needs of foreign buyers. The Fanjing Shan Natural Protected Area in Guizhou Province was set up in 1978 in part to protect the golden monkey. The area has recently been enlarged and declared a Man and Biosphere (MAB) Reserve, an indication of its importance. Wolong Giant Panda Reserve, in the Qionglai Mountains of Sichuan Province, has recently published proposals for the setting up of a captive breeding centre. The plan is to study the golden monkey and help to increase the population of captive animals, thereby reducing the pressure on wild populations from zoos, etc. Although, as yet, there is no reserve that has been specifically established for the species, Happel and Cheek (1986) have suggested that 'refuge areas' (regions to which many rare species, including the golden monkey, retreated during the last ice age), should be designated as protected areas. Suitable regions are the Yunling Mountains of Yunnan Province, the Shennongjia Forest of Hubei Province, and Sichuan Province's Wolong Mountains. This would serve the double purpose of protecting both the golden monkey and the many other rare and endangered species that co-exist with it. Something very similar has already occurred at Wolong Reserve, where golden monkeys and giant pandas frequent the same general habitat. Here the giant panda was the initial *raison d'être* for establishing the protected area but the golden monkey (and many other species) benefit from the protection afforded by reserve status.

TROPICAL
FORESTS

CHINA HAS A RELATIVELY SMALL AREA UNDER TROPICAL FOREST. THIS vegetation zone covers only the southernmost 2–3 per cent of the country: the southern parts of Yunnan, Guangdong and Fujian Provinces, Guangxi Autonomous Region and Taiwan, and all of Hainan Island and the South Sea islands. Although the smallest of the vegetation zones in China, tropical forest is by far the richest, sustaining a huge number of plant species, many of them indigenous. The hot, rainy climate encourages luxuriant plant growth but, as in the eastern monsoon region, much of the original forest has given way to crops and villages or has been cut down to supply the timber industry, so only a fraction of natural vegetation remains.

There is not a lot to choose between tropical monsoon rainforest and tropical rainforest proper. They are very similar in structure and share many plant and animal species. The monsoon forest, however, being further north, experiences both a rainy and a dry season whereas the rainforest proper enjoys almost continual rain throughout the year. The dry season of the tropical monsoon rainforest starts in November. The temperature then is a pleasant 20°C and the taller trees drop their leaves so that the tree canopy thins and makes the forest lighter and more open. With the onset of the rains in April, the temperature rises to 26.5°C and conditions become 'sticky' as the humidity also increases. Then, the roof of the forest darkens again with the rush of growth and the trees flower and fruit. The

Previous page: Yunnan's tropical forest – high canopied, dense and mysterious.

Above: As human population expands, rice fields and houses replace more and more of the forest cover.

canopy is about 25 m high with isolated emergents topping 35 m. No single species of tree dominates but there is a mix that stands out, mainly families of the Chinaberry (Meliaceae), soapberry (Sapindaceae), mulberry (Moraceae), lime or linden (Tiliaceae), custard apple (Annonaceae), durians (Bombacaceae), the sterculia family (Sterculiaceae), the trumpet creeper or bignonia (Bignoniaceae), and also the lychee (*Litchi chinensis*). Less numerous but typical of the tropical monsoon rainforest are two species in the gurjun family (Dipterocarpaceae), i.e. the stellate-hair vatica (*Vatica astrotricha*) and Kwangsi parashorea (*Parashorea chinensis* var. *kwangsiensis*). Epiphytes, woody climbers (lianas) and buttress-root species are numerous but not as well developed as in the true tropical rainforest.

There is a wealth of endemic plants in the tropical monsoon rainforests – more than 500 species on Hainan Dao Island alone and over 300 in Xishuangbanna Reserve in Yunnan. Among those found on Hainan Island are Hainan meyna (*Meyna hainanensis*), Hainan rosewood (*Dalbergia hainanensis*), Hainan belltree (*Radermachera hainanensis*) and Hainan chaulmoogra tree (*Hydnocarpus hainanensis*). Some are economically important, e.g. the mangosteen (*Garcinia mangostena*), from which drugs, dyes and edible fruit are obtained. Endemic species on the mainland include: naked-flowered tetrameles (*Tetrameles nudiflora*) and hsienmu (*Burretiodendron hsienmu*). The deciduous species include Lebbek albizzia (*Albizia lebbek*), a member of the pea family valued for its timber, Chittagong chickrassy (*Chukrasia tabularis*), a mahogany species, and the kapok or silk cotton tree.

In the tropical rainforest proper it is rainy all year round. Conditions are constant, with the temperature moving little around 25°C and the humidity always being high. Because the trees keep their leaves all year round the forest is dark and the shrub and herbaceous layers are not quite as thick and tangled. The trees grow as straight, cathedral-like pillars, relatively easy to walk among, unlike the choked tangle that is characteristic of secondary forest or 'jungle'. The tropical forest of China has much in common with the rainforest of South-East Asia, not only with respect to the species it contains but also in structure. The canopy layer is taller than the tropical monsoon rainforest, averaging more than 40 m with emergents reaching a height of 60 m. The complexity of this ecosystem defies complete study; thousands of plants and animals cooperate or compete with each other in order to survive, creating a finely balanced equilibrium of interactions. Lianas are especially prolific here compared with the tropical monsoon forest. These woody climbers germinate in deep shade and use the trees as supports to reach the precious light they need in order to mature and propagate. Epiphytes also depend on tall trees for support but they germinate on the tree branches and their long, trailing aerial roots supply the plant with nutrients derived from fallen leaves and other debris. Many epiphytes, notably orchids, produce a host of beautiful blooms that have earned them the name 'gardens in the air'. Saprophytes thrive in the deep shadows of the forest. They have no chlorophyll and, instead of photosynthesizing, they live on decaying vegetable matter. Tropical forests proper abound in fig trees (*Ficus* spp.), breadfruits and jackfruits (*Artocarpus* spp.) and in species of the custard-apple family (Annonaceae) and the sapote family (Sapotaceae). Tropical species of bamboo tend to be taller and much thicker-stemmed than their temperate counterparts. Meso bamboo (*Phyllostachys pubescens*) is a common species which grows to a height of 10 m and produces excellent timber for construction and furniture-making. Its rapid growth from shoot to mature plant (a mere 2 months) lends itself to commercial production.

Many of the animal species of China's tropical zone are found in the forests of Burma, Thailand, Laos and Vietnam. There are Indian elephant (*Elephas maximus bengalensis*) and south China tiger (*Panthera tigris amoyensis*), both now very rare. Other ground-dwelling mammals are guar (*Bos guarus*), a huge, bull-like beast weighing up to 1000 kg, binturong (*Arctictis binturong*) and Indian pangolin (*Manis crassicaudata*). Tree-living mammals include three species of gibbon: the white-browed or Hoolock gibbon (*Hylobates hoolock*), the lar or common gibbon (*H. lar*) – now possibly extinct – and the crested or white-cheeked gibbon (*H. concolor*), also known as the concolor. Other tree-dwellers are red giant flying squirrel (*Callosciurus erythraeus*) and the tiny tree shrew (*Tupaia glis*), both of which are active during the day. The slow loris (*Nycticebus coucang*) is active during the night, its movements characteristically slow as it searches for birds' eggs and insects.

Tropical forest birds are numerous and often colourful. Of the tropical pheasants, the green peafowl (*Pavo muticus*) is particularly beautiful. The males have a plumage similar to the familiar peacock (*Pavo cristatus*), with long tail feathers used in courtship displays, but their necks are bronze rather than blue and their backs are a striking iridescent green. Other birds of the forest are the lesser tree duck (*Dendrocygna javanica*), which nests in tree holes, the grass owl (*Tyto capensis*), which nests in thick grass at the edge of the forest, hornbills, e.g. the Indian pied hornbill (*Anthracoceros malabaricus*) and the great pied hornbill (*Buceros bicornis*), and parrots, e.g. the tiny green and red vernal hanging parrot (*Loriculus vernalis*), which is only 12.5 cm long and sleeps at night hanging from a branch like a bat. Eight species of green pigeon (*Treron* spp.) are found here in the southern forests as well as seven species of pittas (*Pitta* spp.) – small, ground-living birds that search for insects in the undergrowth and weave large, spherical nests among the branches. Locals know pittas as 'seven-coloured thrushes' because they are brilliantly coloured. Drongos, e.g. the lesser racquet-tailed drongo (*Drongo remifer*) and the greater racquet-tailed drongo (*D. paradiseus*), are often seen in mixed-species groups eating insects and nectar.

Among the commonest of tropical forest amphibians are tree frogs (*Rhacophorus* spp.). Found close to streams or forest pools, these small frogs cling easily to leaves and stems by means of suction discs on the tips of their toes. Females secure balls of spawn to the leaves so that, when the tadpoles hatch, they drop directly into the water.

The endemic fauna of tropical China is found more on the islands than on the mainland where the forests extend over several countries. The largest, Hainan Island, boasts the most endemics, e.g. the red-shanked douc monkey (*Pygathrix nemasus*), Eld's deer (*Cervus eldik*), the Hainan flying squirrel (*Petinomys electilis*), the Hainan hare (*Lepus hainanus*), the Hainan tree frog (*Rhacophorus oxycephalus*) and the Hainan hill partridge (*Arborophila ardens*). Taiwanese endemics include the Taiwan macaque (*Macaca clyopis*) and Swinhoe's pheasant (*Lophura swinhoei*).

ELEPHANT

THERE ARE FOUR SUBSPECIES OF ELEPHANT (*Elephas maximus*) IN ASIA AND ALL are endangered. They are: Malayan elephant (*E. m. hirsutus*), Sumatran elephant (*E. m. sumatranus*), Ceylon elephant (*E. m. maximus*) and Indian elephant (*E. m. bengalensis*). The Indian elephant is the subspecies that extends into China.

The Indian elephant is not only prized economically as a beast of burden by many cultures, it is also venerated spiritually by them. Hindus, Buddhists and some minority tribes in southern China revere elephants, especially pale or pink-white individuals. On Mount Emei, a mountain in Sichuan Province sacred to Buddhists, we visited a temple near the foot of the mountain which contained a life-sized statue of an elephant. It was special in being white, having three tusks and in being ridden by the Bodhisattva Pu Xian. The Dai minority group in the Xishuangbanna forests of Yunnan have a tradition of worshipping white elephants, which are considered to be auspicious. Their Wild Elephant Temple exists just for this purpose and the elephant's image is seen here and also in their houses and in personal adornment. Their dance drums are in the shape of an elephant's foot and there is a mountain they call Bright Elephant Mountain. When Mao Zedong became Chairman of Communist China in 1949, the Dais presented him with their most prized gift, a live elephant.

Adult Indian elephants weigh up to 5000 kg and are 250–300 cm in height. Elephants walk on the tips of their toes and so their 'knees' are actually wrists. As the animal walks,

Elephants, especially white ones, are revered by various minority groups and by Buddhists. Ten Thousand Year Temple on Mount Emei houses a life-sized statue of the Bodhisattva Pu Xian riding a mythical three-tusked white elephant.

the soles of its feet expand and this helps the immense weight to be distributed more evenly, easing the pressure on the limb bones. The ears are smaller than those of African elephants and are triangular in shape rather than rounded. Cows and some bulls have only rudimentary tusks while, in most bulls, they are relatively short, less than half the length of those of African elephant bulls. The flexible trunk with its prehensile lip functions as an all-purpose hand, used for grabbing plants taller than the animal and passing them to the mouth, but it is also very sensitive to touch and this makes it useful in checking unfamiliar terrain. The skin bears sweat and sebaceous glands but they have a limited ability to cool the body because elephants have a small surface area to volume ratio, so keeping cool in a hot climate is not easy. This is where large thin pieces of anatomy, namely the ears, prove useful. These are flapped about when the weather is particularly hot and, together with mud and water baths, are very effective in keeping the animal cool. Both sexes have cheek glands between the eyes and ears which open to the surface through slits in the skin. Cheek glands are rarely active in cows (in contrast to the situation in African elephant females) but, in bulls, they periodically secrete a dark, strong-smelling fluid. Bulls can be 'in musth' for several hours or several months at a time and, during this period, they mark trees with their cheek glands and are very aggressive, especially towards other bulls. They mate more frequently than other bulls when in musth, although they can also mate outside of musth.

RANGE The Indian elephant ranges from southern and eastern India through Burma, Thailand, Laos and Vietnam into Yunnan Province in China. Here, they are confined to the tropical forests of Xishuangbanna although there is evidence to suggest that they were once spread over a much larger area of eastern China.

HABITAT Like the other three species of Asian elephant the Indian elephant lives in tropical rainforest. The African elephant is, by contrast, a savannah-dwelling species.

BEHAVIOUR For such a large animal, elephants move remarkably quietly through the forest and entire herds may go unnoticed until they are actually spotted. In the forests of Yunnan, they travel along well-trodden paths in family groups of three of four or in herds of 40–50 individuals. Herds consist of an adult male and a number of females with two or three generations of young. The very young are kept in the middle of the group surrounded by cows. Elephants on their own are usually old males or males that are disabled in some way or other.

Home ranges, especially of the bigger herds, are large, covering many square kilometres, and the residents exploit them in cyclical fashion, effectively allowing feeding areas time to recover. Herds often travel 30 km in a single day although, if young calves are present, they move only 1–2 km a day through the best feeding sites. An adult consumes 50–200 kg or more of plant material and almost 100 litres of water every day. Grasses, roots, bark, fruits, Bajoa banana leaves, palm leaves, bamboo leaves and bamboo shoots are all grist to this herbivore's mill. Journalist Tang Xiyang also describes the elephant's predilection for a

Opposite: Unlike its African cousin, the Indian elephant (*Elephas maximus bengalensis*) is a creature of the forest.

certain species of palm tree. He does not name the species but it apparently grows tall and is 6–9 cm in diameter.

The elephant generally first sprays the roots of the tree with water from its trunk, then tramples the earth and bumps against the tree until it is able to pull it down with its trunk, strip off the bark and get at the pulp.

There has been little work done on the Chinese populations of Indian elephant but a study carried out by Indian biologist R. Sukumar (1990) in southern India throws some light on the feeding habits of local populations. Sukumar found that, while elephants ate 112 plant species in the study area, most of what they ate (85 per cent) consisted of only 25 species from four families, namely the Leguminosae, Palmae, Cyperaceae and Gramineae, and from the order Malvales. Herds browsed on shrubs and trees during the dry season and changed to a grass diet during the early part of the wet season. This changing diet maximized the protein intake. Raids on village crops were only sporadic in the dry season but increased in the wet season to plague proportions, occurring almost every night. At this time of year villagers plant out more land in crops, mainly cereals and millet, and this new growth contains more protein, calcium and sodium than wild grasses, hence its attraction to the local elephant herds. Of their total annual food requirements, adult bull elephants derived about 9.3 per cent by weight from cropland while females derived about 1.7 per cent. Sukumar concludes that crop raiding is part of the elephant's optimal foraging strategy.

Elephants eat huge quantities of food not only because they have to sustain a large body but also because their digestion is very inefficient. As much as half their food passes through the gut undigested. They are forced to spend most of the day eating with less than 4 hours sleeping.

Elephant cows first breed at about 10 years of age and they can bear young throughout their lifetime, which means that a female can breed for 25 years of more. Theoretically, this means that females could produce a maximum of about 13 young but, in practice, she will produce only half this number. Various factors are responsible for this. First of all, only half of all young elephants make it to sexual maturity. Moreover, a female usually becomes pregnant only once every 5 or 6 years and bears only a single calf. Pregnancy is also long, about 20–22 months.

The cohesiveness of elephant herds and the strength of social bonds is at no time better observed than at birth. The herd forms a protective ring around the pregnant female and some cows will actually act as midwives, cleaning the infant and helping it to stand. The calf is able to move with the herd less than an hour later. At 1 m in height, it barely reaches its mother's lower thigh and weighs a modest 90 kg or so, one-fiftieth of her weight. It suckles for up to 6 months although it does partake of plant food long before this, helped by its mother or other members of the herd. In order to allow mothers time to feed and meet their substantial calorie needs, young elephants are grouped together in a crèche in the middle of the herd and are looked after by baby-sitters. These may be older brothers or sisters or a relation of some sort.

Above: The social bond between mother and infant Indian elephant is very strong.

Overleaf: Water-holes are important both for drinking and for keeping the elephant cool.

STATUS It is estimated that there are fewer than 12 000 of this subspecies left in the wild and the Chinese populations are particularly highly endangered – only 200 remain. The problem is primarily one of habitat loss leading to homelessness and lack of food and, ultimately, to crop damage. These problems have become more critical in recent decades but they existed as long ago as the 1500s. Ming-Dynasty author Li Wenfeng describes one such situation in his *Moon and Mountain Collection*:

> In 1547, in the reign of the Ming Dynasty Jiajing emperor, herds of elephants from Dalian Mountain trampled people's crops. Attempts to drive them away failed. Hu Ao, the county magistrate, and local officials led the villagers in an expedition to catch the elephants. They created a fence of wooden boards three metres long held up by several people. As soon as the elephants entered the area of encirclement, the villagers closed the fence. Arrows were shot and spears hurled from a trench outside the fence to prevent the elephants from breaking out and running away. Then the villagers set fire to the area, for the elephants could not stand the heat. In this way they captured some dozen elephants.

Today, there are laws in China against killing or capturing elephants but they are still effectively killed through deforestation for timber and agriculture. Every year about 300 km² of forest in Xishuangbanna are destroyed. Various minority groups, e.g. Dai, Yao, Hani and Jinuo, as well as Han Chinese, inhabit the forest and its environs, most living a nomadic slash-and-burn existence and a few actually living as hunter-gatherers deep in the forests. When we visited Xishuangbanna Nature Reserve in 1984 we found evidence of elephants in secondary growth close to the fields of a Dai village. We saw droppings and were taken to a clay pit scoured with tusk marks where the elephants obtained salts and minerals. Our guides carried Kalashnikov rifles and warned us to be very careful as the elephants were known to be dangerous. Their heightened aggression suggested an intolerable encroachment of their habitat by human beings, a situation confirmed by accounts of elephants raiding the crops of villagers.

CONSERVATION MEASURES Various measures have been carried out to give backing to the legal protection of the Indian elephant in China. We were told that farmers are given compensation for the loss of their crops and that the zone of fields and secondary forest bordering the rainforest proper was used as a buffer zone. Against this, forestry operations in parts of Xishuangbanna Reserve continue to put pressure on a dwindling habitat. Realistically, it is difficult to see how clear-fell logging and elephant conservation can be reconciled. Given the amount of forest left, these operations should cease immediately if the elephant population is to remain viable. Alternative means of earning income for locals and the provincial government should be looked at. Many minority groups, such as Dais, revere elephants and the forest itself and, in many sacred areas, it is a spiritual offence to cut trees down. It may well be worthwhile to explore the idea of reinforcing and extending such traditions for the long-term benefit of both elephant and forest.

GIBBONS

Two species of gibbon inhabit the southern periphery of South-West China, the concolor gibbon (of which there are two subspecies, *Hylobates concolor leucogenys* and *H. c. concolor*) and the Hoolock gibbon (*H. hoolock*). A third species, the lar gibbon (*H. lar carpenteri*) has also been recorded in China, but no recent sightings have been reported and many authorities regard it as extinct within the borders of the People's Republic.

One of the most northerly ranging of the gibbon family (Hylobatidae), the concolor gibbon (also known as the crested gibbon) is one of the lightest of the group, weighing no more than 6 kg. The sexes are similar in appearance, with the long arms, upright posture and lack of

Of all the apes, the gibbon is the most specialized for brachiation (swinging from each arm alternately).

tail typical of all gibbons. Pelt colour shows sexual dimorphism. Infant concolor gibbons are born white, irrespective of sex but, as they approach adulthood, the males become jet black, except for white cheek patches, while adult females are transformed into a beautiful dusky gold, except for a black patch on the crown of the head. As well as the white cheek patches, the peak or crest of hair on the head and the shape of the nose, make concolor gibbons easy to differentiate from other gibbon species. Moreover, the male's throat sac (used to amplify his vocalizations) is much smaller than those of other species.

The Hoolock gibbon is similar in appearance to *H. concolor*, the male being black and the female golden, but both sexes possess distinctive white 'eyebrows', accounting for its common name, 'white-browed gibbon'.

RANGE The concolor gibbon's range covers most of Vietnam and parts of Laos, although it is nowhere common. In China, *H. concolor* was once found over a wide area: 1000 years ago the species was reported as far north as the Yellow River (Huang He), just 600 km south of present-day Beijing. By the seventeenth century the gibbons' range had contracted to a point midway between the Yangtze (Chang Jiang) and the Sikiang River systems. Numbers and range steadily declined but, even early this century, the animal could be found from the China/Vietnam border northwards to the banks of the Sikiang River. Nowadays, the two subspecies are confined to a small area in the south of Yunnan Province. *H. c. leucogenys* occurs in the extreme south of the province, while *H. c. concolor* is found in south-eastern Yunnan and Hainan Island (Sung & Guoqiang, 1986).

The Hoolock gibbon is distributed in south-western Yunnan, while the lar gibbon (if it exists at all) is restricted to small areas of extreme south-western Yunnan.

HABITAT The deciduous monsoon forests of Yunnan are composed of two main types: tropical semi-evergreen and tropical moist deciduous forests. These forests contain a huge variety of tree species, of which fig trees (*Ficus* spp.) would seem to be of most importance to the gibbon.

BEHAVIOUR Gibbon society would bring a glow of satisfaction to human beings who venerate family life as the bedrock of social stability. With their close relatives, the siamangs, gibbons are the only apes to practise monogamy. All gibbon species live in 'nuclear families', comprising a monogamous male and female unit with their dependent offspring, numbering up to four and ranging from infants (newborn to 2 years old), through juveniles of 2–4 years old, to adolescents of 4–6 years old. Adolescents have almost cut the gibbon equivalent of apron-strings and feed and forage on the periphery of the family group.

The 'family' holds an area of rainforest which it defends from other gibbons in two main ways: by calling and by vigorous tree-top displays. Calling is usually initiated by the female and comprises a series of rising notes, extremely evocative to people who have heard its pure tones carrying far over the tree canopy at dawn but holding a far more prosaic 'Keep Off' significance to other gibbon families. When two families do meet at the border

Opposite: Incongruously, the adult female black gibbon possesses a golden pelt.

of their territories, physical displays often alternate with calling. The adults (and occasionally juveniles) swing and crash through the branches in a madcap display that seems to be intended to impress observers with the gibbon equivalent of saying: 'Look, I am fit and agile and full of energy; you are wasting your time if you think you can muscle in on my territory. Don't even try it.'

These contests occasionally become tests of endurance, with neither side willing to concede defeat. Unlike calling, the male often takes the initiative with displays. Ellefson (1974) describes one such conflict in his study of white-handed gibbons (*Hylobates lar*). The male:

> . . . gives soft calls when he sees the neighbouring group; the two males sit watching each other. During the next 70 minutes this staring alternates with conflict-hooting, acrobatic displays and one or two chases to and fro across the boundary [between the two families' territories]. There is no apparent victory or gain. The other members of the group tire long before the males and move back to their respective territories to rest and forage.

Such territorial disputes are inevitable. The gibbon is almost totally arboreal; it has to obtain from the tree canopy everything it needs to survive. So each gibbon family must 'own' sufficient trees for its requirements. With their ability to hang beneath tree limbs for long periods, the species seems to be adapted to the 'terminal branch' niche, where they can collect fruit, flowers and protein-rich new leaves with an ease denied any other primate. The products of fig trees seem to form a high percentage of the diet. With many species of *Ficus* in a given area, each having a short flowering cycle and bursting into bloom independent of other trees, food is continuously available to the gibbon. Gibbons do, however, feed on whatever species of edible tree is available, taking leaves, shoots, berries and fruit, and supplementing their diet with the occasional insect.

STATUS All gibbon species in China have suffered from deforestation and degradation of their habitat. In China, the concolor gibbon is thought to be endangered, although no estimate of its total numbers are available on the mainland. Ma and Wang (1988) claim that the population is 'increasing slightly'. The tiny relict population of *H. concolor* still surviving precariously on Hainan Island is believed to number no more than 12 animals. In the 1950s, this group of island-living gibbons was estimated at 2000 individuals.

The Hoolock gibbon is in similar straits, being classified as critically endangered (Sung & Guoqiang, 1986). The lar gibbon has seldom been encountered in recent years and its continued survival in China has been questioned.

CONSERVATION MEASURES All species of gibbon are categorized as Class 1 protected animals. No specific conservation projects are extant for any of these species. However, the concolor gibbon is found in seven established nature reserves, the Hoolock and the lar in one reserve each, and this should confer some limited measure of security on these beautiful and fascinating primates.

EPILOGUE

THIS BOOK HAS BEEN ABLE TO DETAIL ONLY A FEW OF THE MORE REMARKABLE and beautiful of China's threatened species. Scores of others – Eld's deer on Hainan Island, Chinese sturgeon, Sichuan hill partridge, brown-eared pheasant, argali, black-necked crane, gaur (the list is almost endless) – all, for reasons of space, have had to be omitted. Exercising choice in these matters leaves one feeling more than slightly uneasy. On what criteria do we include an animal? What constitutes 'remarkableness' or 'beauty'? And is beauty a valid criterion for inclusion or, in another context, for conservation?

The giant panda is 'saveworthy' because it is beautiful; so is the tiger, the crested ibis and the snow leopard. But is that sufficient reason? The answer seems to be: probably not. We are all too human in our decisions; many people will shed tears if a whale species is blotted out but who will man the barricades to prevent the extinction of a spider? At a very visceral level we agree with Keats' dangerous concept that beauty is truth (and by extension goodness), and with its corollary: ugliness equals falsehood (and therefore evil). Consciously or subconsciously, ugly/evil creatures are far more easily dispensed with than the species we perceive as beautiful/good. This is why the panda *must* at all costs be saved, while the *Megaphrys* frog excites no passionate protectors.

This *gestalt* may be inevitable but we can overcome its worst failings by recognizing the fallibility of our feelings and using those species we cannot choose but love as symbolic of the habitat in which they live. If we wish to save our planet's diversity it cannot be stressed too often that habitat is all. Indeed, loving the panda as an entity separate from its environment is the height of folly: the panda cannot survive as a panda without its environment, unless existence as a zoo-bred automaton, whose only function is to entertain bored urbanites on wet Sunday afternoons, can be classified as 'survival'.

Do the species described in this book (and their habitats) stand a chance of surviving into the foreseeable future? If enough protected habitat is available, the prognosis must be good. Certainly, endangered animals in China are at least as well off as anywhere else on the surface of the globe. In the past 30 years the number of designated nature reserves in China has increased at an impressive rate. To date these protected areas now number more than 800 reserves, including 57 at national level, and covering a total of 440 000 km². This is equivalent to about 5 per cent of the land area, an extremely healthy figure (Britain's percentage is under 3 per cent). However, in manpower terms, China's wildlife policy still has some way to go. The number of wildlife management officials at national level in China is 200, while in the USA, for example, the equivalent figure is 1200.

As in most other countries, over-exploitation of forests and other ecosystems continues to have an impact on these areas and to erode some of the gains made. But, in one extremely important way, Chinese endangered species are far better off than those in most other, non-Western countries.

Overpopulation has recently become a respectable topic of conversation and people now worry about the great difficulty (some would say impossibility) of feeding the world's projected human population even 30 years hence. What seems to be forgotten is that, before the worst Malthusian horrors of overpopulation are visited upon the human race, all available space will be filled by teeming billions of *Homo sapiens*. What price then 'endangered species'? Wilderness areas, nature reserves and World Heritage Sites, all will be swept away before the irresistible tide of human increase. Talk of bio-diversity, even of 'tourist dollars', will mean nothing to men or women desperately attempting to feed a starving child. And before human numbers crash in disease, famine and despair, they will, locust-like, have stripped their environment of even the smallest place where wildlife can survive. Those people that survive through such catastrophes will live in a sterile, impoverished world, devoid of the wondrous vibrant diversity that former generations had taken for granted. Unlike, for example, India, Kenya, or other countries with their own, justifiable claim to wildlife fame, China seized the nettle of population control decades ago. Though far from perfect in its implementation, the 'one-child-one-family' policy has produced a pronounced decrease in China's fertility rate (down from 6.25 in 1951 to 2.25 in 1982, while Latin America's has reduced from 6 to 4 and Africa's continues to hover around 6.25). If adhered

This billboard in Chengdu persuades couples to adhere to the one-child policy by underlining the financial gains made, and the better lifestyle achieved, by population control.

to, this ability to curb human population growth will probably do as much as any other single factor to save China's threatened wildlife (and to enhance the quality of life of the human population also).

The future is by no means secure. The Chinese have a history of appreciation of the natural world; their major religions and many of their artistic values are nature-oriented. They are already primed, culturally, for the conservation ethic. However, newer values are being enthusiastically absorbed. China is industrializing with prodigious speed and with modernization comes heightened aspirations for material well-being. Like every other country in the world, most Chinese look with longing towards the 'Golden Mountain', the USA, and wish to emulate the lifestyle of America's well-to-do. If China's billion-plus people absorbed resources at even half the rate of the mega-wasteful American consumer then, population control or not, eco-disaster will be just around the corner. Yet, why should the Chinese deny themselves if the USA (and to a lesser extent western Europe) will not? And what politician, in the market-led, consumer-choice Free World, will face the voters with a message of abstinence, fewer cars, less jet travel, reduced consumer choice, a complete change of life-style?

Without such a change of aspirations, however, for the West to pontificate on how other countries should manage their portion of this globe is hypocritical in the extreme. Hypocritical, but realistic? Perhaps the whole idea of reduced consumption is impracticable; perhaps the human brain is pre-programmed with an irresistible desire to beat our neighbours, to climb to the top of the heap, to have the biggest, the best, the most of everything. Perhaps this is what has brought us so far, so fast. And yet, and yet. Human beings are not an unintelligent species, or so we like to believe. We have bestowed upon ourselves the title *Homo sapiens*, 'Wise Man'. We have the gift of foresight and can, in theory, see which way our desires are leading us. If we foresee destruction, for the natural world now and, ultimately, for ourselves, surely Wise Man is sufficiently intelligent to choose a safer course. It is time humanity began living up to its self-given title.

A change in lifestyle in the West could materially affect China's attitude to its own modernization programme, to its own aspirations. It may be impracticable, it is probably idealistic, but expectations in the West could tip the balance one way or the other. Put another way, your own desire for cars, travel, food and clothing may well decide, through a long chain of cause and effect, whether the panda lives or dies.

FURTHER READING

PREFACE

Laidler, K. & Laidler, L. (1992) *Pandas – Giants of the Bamboo Forest*. BBC Books, London.

Schaller, G.B., Hu, J., Pan, W. & Zhu, J. (1985) *The Giant Pandas of Wolong*. University of Chicago Press, Chicago.

Tang, X. (1987) *Living Treasures. An Odyssey through China's Extraordinary Nature Reserves*. Bantam Books Inc. and New World Press.

Zhao, J., Zheng, G., Wang, H. & Xu, J. (1990) *The Natural History of China*. Collins & Sons Co. Ltd, London.

CHINA: A WORLD OF ITS OWN

Archibald, G.A. (1987) 'Eight years of collaboration between China and the International Crane Foundation in the conservation of cranes and wetlands.' Paper presented at the International Conference on Wildlife Conservation in China, Beijing, July 1987. Mimeograph.

Chen, G. (1985) 'China establishes more nature reserves.' *Biol. Conserv.*, vol. 31, pp. 1–5.

Meng, S. (1990) 'China's nature reserves: preserving her wildlife heritage.' *China Today*, Feb., pp. 12–13.

Meng, S. (1993) 'The human race and the world of nature: live and let live.' *China Today*, Sept., pp. 12–13.

Schaller, G.B. (1993) *The Last Panda*. University of Chicago Press, Chicago.

USSR Academy of Sciences, Institute of Geography (1969) *The Physical Geography of China*. Frederick Praeger, London.

Wang, S. & MacKinnon, J. (1993) 'Urgent recommendations to save China's biological diversity: report to the Chinese Council for International Cooperation in Environment and Development (CCICED).' *Chinese Biodiversity*, vol. 1, pp. 2–13.

Xu, X. (1987) 'Wildlife management in China.' Paper presented at the International Conference on Wildlife Conservation in China, Beijing, July 1987. Mimeograph.

Zhao, J., Zheng, G., Wang, H. & Xu, J. (1990) *The Natural History of China*. Collins & Sons Co. Ltd, London.

NORTHERN FORESTS AND WETLANDS

Red-crowned crane

Anon. (1983) *The Red-crowned Crane*. China Pictorial Press, Beijing.

Ma, Y. & Jin, L. (1987) 'The numerical distribution of the red-crowned crane in Sanjiang Plain area of Heilongjiang Province, China.' *Acta. Zool. Sin.*, vol. 33, no. 1, pp. 82–7.

Ma, Y. & Li, X. (1987) 'The numerical distribution of red-crowned crane in China.' Paper presented at the International Conference on Wildlife Conservation in China, Beijing, July 1987. Mimeograph.

Ma, Y., Jin, L., Jin, A & Fu, C. (1987) 'An aerial survey of red-crowned cranes and other rare waders in the Wuyurhe River Basin of Heilongjiang Province, China.' *Acta. Zool. Sin.*, vol. 33, no. 2, pp. 187–91.

Manchurian tiger

Li, W. (1990) 'Changbai Mountain Nature Reserve.' *China Today*, Feb., pp. 12–13.

Sidenius, D. (1993) 'For the south China tiger, it's now or never.' *China Today*, Sept., pp. 28–30.

DESERTS AND LOWLAND STEPPES

Przewalski's horse

Gao, X. Gu, J. (1989) 'The distribution and status of the Equidae in China.' *Acta. Theriol. Sin.*, vol. 9, no. 4, pp. 269–74.

Sokolov, V.E., Amarsanaa, G., Paklina, N.V., Pozdnyakova, M.K., Rachkovskaya, E.I. & Kotolkhuu, N. (1991) 'Range of *Equus prezewalskii* in the last period of this species' existence in Mongolia and its geobotanic characteristics.' *Zool. Zh.*, vol. 70, no. 5, pp. 111–16.

Sokolov, V.E., Dulamtseren, S., Orlov, V.N. & Kotolkhuu, N. (1980) 'Current state and problems of perissodactyls of the Great Gobi Reserve, Mongolia.' *Problemy Ocvocniya Pusty*, no. 5, pp. 76–9. *Problems of Desert Development*, no. 5, pp. 77–81.

WWF (1982) 'Europe: establishment of semi-reserves for Przewalski's horse.' *WWF-UK Rep. Project 9E0023*.

Bactrian camel

Bannikov, A. (1976) 'Wild camels of the Gobi.' *Wildlife*, vol. 18, pp. 398–403.

Przewalski, N. (1879) *From Kula across the Tian Shan to Lob Nor*. Sampson Low, Marston, Seale & Rivington.

Tulgat, Y., & Schaller, G.B. (1992) *Biol. Conserv.*, vol. 62, no. 1, pp. 11–19.

QINGHAI-TIBET PLATEAU: UPLAND STEPPES

O'Gara, B. (1987) 'Harvesting of Qinghai ungulates.' Paper presented at the International Conference on Wildlife Conservation in China, Beijing, July 1987. Mimeograph.

Snow leopard

Jackson, R. & Ahlborn, G. (1989) 'Snow leopards, *Panthera uncia*, in Nepal: home range and movements.' *Nat. Geogr. Res.*, vol. 5, no. 2, pp. 161–75.

Liao, Y. (1985) 'The geographical distribution of ounces, *Panthera uncia*, in Qinghai Province, China.' *Acta Theriol. Sin.*, vol. 5, no. 3, pp. 183–8.

Liao, Y., Luo, H. Liou, D., Xu, S., & Yuan, B. (1986) 'A preliminary study of the rearing and breeding of snow leopard, *Panthera uncia.' Acta Theriol. Sin.*, vol. 6, no. 2, pp. 93–100.

Oli, M.K., Taylor, I.R. & Rogers, M.E. (1993) 'Diet of the snow leopard, *Panthera uncia* in the Annapurna Conservation Area, Nepal.' *J. Zool. Lond.*, vol. 231, no. 3, pp. 365–70.

Oli, M.K., Taylor, I.R. & Rogers, M.E. (1994) 'Snow leopard, *Panthera uncia*, predation of livestock: an assessment of local perceptions in the Annapurna Conservation Area, Nepal.' *Biol. Conserv.*, vol. 68, no. 1, pp. 63–8.

Schaller, G.B., Junrang, R. & Mingjiang, Q. (1988) 'Status of the snow leopard, *Panthera uncia*, in Qinghai and Gansu Provinces, China.' *Biol. Conserv.*, vol. 45, no. 3, pp. 179–94.

Schaller, G.B., Hong, L., Junrang, T.R. & Mingjiang, Q. (1988) 'The snow leopard in Xinjiang, China.' *Oryx*, vol. 22, no. 4, pp. 197–204.

Schaller, G.B., Talipu, L.H., Hua, L., Junrang, R., Mingjiang, Q. & Haibin, W. (1987) 'Status of large mammals in the Taxkorgan Reserve, Xinjiang, China.' *Biol. Conserv.*, vol. 42, pp. 53–71.

Shah, K.B. (1989) 'On a hunting pair of snow leopards in western Nepal.' *J. Bombay Nat. Hist. Soc.*, vol. 86, no. 2, pp. 236–7.

Wild ass

Chu, G., Liang, C., Ruan, Y., Wang, W. & Hou, H. (1985) 'The summer habitat and population numbers of the Mongolian wild ass, *Equus hemionus hemionus*, in the Kalamaili Mountains Wildlife Reserve, Xinjiang-Uygur Autonomous Region, China.' *Acta Zool. Sin.*, vol. 31, no. 2, pp. 178–86.

Gao, X. & Gu. J. (1989) 'The distribution and status of the Equidae in China.' *Acta Theriol. Sin.*, vol. 9, no. 4, pp. 269–74.

Groves, C. (1974) *Horses of the World*. David and Charles.

Sokolov, V.E., Dulamtseren, S., Orlov, V.N. & Kotolkhuu, N. (1980) 'Current state and problems of perissodactyls of the Great Gobi Reserve, Mongolia.' *Problemy Ocvocniya Pustyn*, no. 5, pp. 76–9. *Problems of Desert Development*, no. 5, pp. 77–81.

White-lipped deer

Cai, G. (1988) 'Notes on white-lipped deer, *Cervus albirostris*, in China.' *Acta Theriol. Sin.*, vol. 8, no. 1, pp. 7–12.

Feng, Z., Zheng, C. & Cai, G. (1980) 'Mammals from the southeastern Xizang (Tibet).' *Acta Zool. Sin.*, vol. 26, no. 1, pp. 91–7.

Jaczewski, Z., (1986) 'Some data on Thorold's deer, *Cervus albirostris*'. *Z. Jagdewiss.*, vol. 32, no. 2, pp. 75–83.

Kaji, K. Ohtaishi, N. Miura, S. & Wu, J. (1989) 'Distribution and status of the white-lipped deer, *Cervus albirostris*, in the Qinghai-Tibet Plateau, China.' *Mammal Rev.*, vol. 19, no. 1, pp. 35–44.

Miura, S. et al. (1989) 'White-lipped deer in China.' *Biol. Conserv.*, vol. 47, pp. 237–44.

Oswald, C. & Jaczewski, Z. (1985) 'Some data about Thorold's deer, *Cervus albirostris*.' *Przegl. Zool.*, vol. 29, no. 2, pp. 215–16.

Schaller, G.B., Junrang, R. & Mingjiang, Q. (1988) 'Status of the snow leopard, *Panthera uncia*, in Qinghai and Gansu Provinces, China.' *Biol. Conserv.*, vol. 45, no. 3, pp. 179–94.

Schaller, G.B., Talipu, L.H. Hua, L., Junrang, R., Mingjiang, Q. & Haibin, W. (1987) 'Status of large mammals in the Taxkorgan Reserve, Xinjiang, China.' *Biol. Conserv.*, vol. 42, pp. 53–71.

Zheng, S., Wu, J. & Han, Y. (1989) 'Preliminary investigation on the food habits and reproduction of the white-lipped deer.' *Acta Theriol. Sin.*, vol. 9, no. 2, pp. 123–9.

Yak

Przewalski, N.M. (1876) *Mongolia, the Tangut Country, and the Solitudes of Northern Tibet*. London.

Rockhill, W. (1891) 'The land of the lamas: notes of a journey through China, Mongolia and Tibet.'

Schaefer, E. (1951) *Grande Chasses sur le Toit du Monde*. Paris.

Schaller, G.B. (1993) 'Tibet: remote Chang Tang.' *Natnl Geographic*, Aug., pp. 62–87.

Tibetan antelope

Schaller, G.B. (1993) 'Tibet: remote Chang Tang.' *Natnl Geographic*, Aug., pp. 62–87.

EASTERN PLAINS AND YANGTZE WETLANDS

Chinese alligator

Chen, B. (1987) 'An analysis of the changes in geographical distribution of the Chinese alligator.' (Department of Biology, Anhui Normal University, Anhui, China.) Paper presented at the International Conference on Wildlife Conservation in China, Beijing, July 1987. Mimeograph.

Huang, Z. & Watanabe, M.E. (1987) 'Nest excavation and hatching behaviours of Chinese alligator and American alligator.' (Institute of Zoology, Academia Sinica; National academy of Sciences, USA.) Paper presented at the International Conference on Wildlife Conservation in China, Beijing, July 1987. Mimeograph.

Huang, Z., Lin, H. & Zhang, S. (1986) 'Analysis of the LANDSAT remote sensing images of the types of habitat of the Yangtse alligators.' *Chinese J. Oceanol. Limnol.*, vol. 4, no. 4, pp. 360–71.

Tang, X. (1987) *Living Treasures. An Odyssey through China's Extraordinary Nature Reserves*. Bantam Books Inc. and New World Press.

Yangtze dolphin

Deng, S. (1993) The panda of the Yangtse River.' *China Today*, vol. 42, no. 7, pp. 49–52.

Han, C. (1982) 'The status of research on the Chinese river dolphin, *Lipotes vexillifer* in China.' *Acta Theriol. Sin.*, vol. 2, no. 2, pp. 245–52.

Kaiya, Z., Pilleri, G. & Yuemin, L. (1979) 'Observations on the baiji, *Lipotes vexillifer*, and the finless porpoise, *Neophocaena asiaeorientalis*, in the Changjiang (Yangtse) River between Nanjing and Taiyangzhou, China, with remarks on some physiological adaptations of the baiji to its environment.' *Invest. Cetacea*, vol. 10, pp. 109–20.

Kaiya, Z., Pilleri, G. & Li., Y. (1980) 'Observations on the baiji, *Lipotes vexillifer*, and the finless porpoise, *Neophocaena asiaeorientalis*, in the Changjiang (Yangtse) River between Nanjing and Taiyangzhou, China, with remarks on some physiological adaptations of the baiji to its environment.' *Scientia Sin.*, vol. 23, no. 6, pp. 785–95.

Liu, R. (1987) '*Lipotes* research in the Institute of Hydrobiology, Academia Sinica, Wuhan.' (Institute of Hydrobiology, Academia Sinica.) Paper presented at the International Conference on Wildlife Conservation in China, Beijing, July 1987. Mimeograph.

Peixun, C., Peilin, L., Renjun, L., Kejie, L. & Pilleri, G. (1979) 'Distribution, ecology, behaviour and conservation of the dolphins of the Changjiang (Yangtse) River, Wuhan-Yueyang, China. *Invest. Cetacea*, vol. 10, pp. 87–104.

Wang, X. (1987) 'Conservation of precious and rare aquatic animals in China.' Paper presented at the International Conference on Wildlife Conservation in China, Beijing, July 1987. Mimeograph.

Zhou, K. (1986a) 'An outline of marine mammalogical researches in China.' *Acta Theriol. Sin.*, vol. 6, no. 3, pp. 219–32.

Zhou, K. (1986b) 'A project to translocate the baiji, *Lipotes vexillifer*, from the main stream of the Yangtze River, China, to Tongling Baiji Nature Reserve.' *Aquatic Mammals*, vol. 12, no. 1, pp. 21–4.

Zhou, K. (1987) 'A semi-natural reserve for baiji at Tongling.' (Department of Biology, Nanjing Normal University, Nanjing, China.) Paper presented at the International Conference on Wildlife Conservation in China, Beijing, July 1987. Mimeograph.

Giant salamander

Song, M. (1988) 'The study of growth in the Chinese giant salamander.' In: Matsui, M., Hikida, T. & Goris, R.C. (eds) *Current Herpetology in East Asia*. Second Japan-China Herpetological Symposium, Kyoto, Japan, July 1988.

Père David's deer

Wang, S. (1987) 'An overview of the recent progress in wildlife research and conservation in China.' Paper presented at the International Conference on Wildlife Conservation in China, Beijing, July 1987. Mimeograph.

WWF (1993) 'China: habitat assessment and re-introduction of Père David's deer.' *WWF-UK Rep. Project CN009*. 2 pp.

CHINA'S LOST WORLDS: MONTANE TEMPERATE FORESTS

Chen, L. (1988a) 'The tree everyone thought extinct.' *China Reconstructs*, Jul., p. 41.

Chen, L. (1988b) '*Cathaya argyrophylla* – "giant panda" of plants.' *China Reconstructs*, Nov., p. 28.

Tang, X. (1987) *Living Treasures. An Odyssey through China's Extraordinary Nature Reserves*. Bantam Books Inc. and New World Press.

Giant panda

De Wulf, R., MacKinnon, J.R. & Cai, W.S. (1988) 'Remote sensing for wildlife management: giant panda habitat mapping from LANDSAT MSS images.' *Geocarto International*, no. 1, pp. 41–50.

Laidler, K. & Laidler, L. (1992) *Pandas – Giants of the Bamboo Forest*. BBC Books, London.

Reid, D.G., Taylor, A.H., Hu, J. & Qin, Z. (1991) 'Environmental influences on bamboo, *Bashania fangiana*, growth and implications for giant panda conservation.' *J. Appl. Ecol.*, vol. 28, no. 3, pp. 855–68.

Schaller, G.B. (1993) *The Last Panda*. University of Chicago Press, Chicago.

Schaller, G.B., Hu, J., Pan, W. & Zhu, J. (1985) *The Giant Pandas of Wolong*. University of Chicago Press, Chicago.

Taylor, A.H. (1993) 'Bamboo regeneration after flowering in the Wolong Giant Panda Reserve, China.' *Biol. Conserv.*, vol. 63, no. 3, pp. 231–4.

Red panda

Glaston, A.R. (1994) *The Red or Lesser Panda Studbook, No. 8*. Stichting Koninklijke Rotterdaamse Diergaarde, Rotterdam.

Johnson, K.G., Schaller, G.B. & Hu, J. (1988) 'Comparative behaviour of red and giant pandas in the Wolong Reserve, China.' *J. Mammal.*, vol. 69, no. 3, pp. 552–64.

Laidler, K. & Laidler, L. (1992) *Pandas – Giants of the Bamboo Forest*. BBC Books, London.

Reid, D.G., Jinchu, H. & Yan, H. (1991) 'Ecology of the red panda, *Ailurus fulgens*, in the Wolong Reserve, China.' *J. Zool. Lond.*, vol. 225, no. 3, pp. 347–64.

Roberts, M. & Kessler, D. (1979) 'Reproduction in red pandas, *Ailurus fulgens* (Carnivora: Ailuropodidae).' *J. Zool. Lond.*, vol. 188, pp. 235–49.

Takin

Chapman Andrews, R. (1924) 'The quest of the golden fleece. II. Takin on their rugged peaks.' *Asia*, pp. 515–68.

Ge, T., Jiang, M. & Deng, O. (1989) 'The herd compositions, numbers and distribution of Sichuan takin, *Budorcas taxicolor tibetana*, in Tangjiahe Nature Reserve, China.' *Acta Theriol. Sin.*, vol. 9, no. 4, pp. 262–8.

Groves, P. (1992) 'Aspects of golden takin ecology in the Qinling Mountains, China.' Paper presented at the First Arctic Ungulate Conference, Nuuk, Greenland, 3–8 September 1991. *Rangifer*, vol. 12, no. 3, pp. 161–3.

Schaller, G.B., Teng, Q., Pan, W., Qin, Z., Wang, X., Hu, J. & Shen, H. (1986) 'Feeding behaviour of Sichuan takin, *Budorcas taxicolor*.' *Mammalia*, vol. 50, no. 3, pp. 311–22.

Wu, J. (1986) 'Study of system and distribution of Chinese takin, *Budorcas taxicolor*.' *Dongwuxue Yanjiu*, vol. 7, no. 2, pp. 167–75.

Wu, J., Han. Y., Yong, Y. & Zhao, J. (1987) 'Preliminary study of food habits and character of population of Chinese takin.' (Shaanxi Institute of Zoology; Shaanxi Fuping Reserve.) Paper presented at the International Conference on Wildlife Conservation in China, Beijing, July 1987. Mimeograph.

Crested ibis

Hadfield, P. (1994) 'If you can't save them, freeze them.' *New Scient.* (*This Week*, 29 Jan.), p. 10.

Li, F. (1991) 'World's first captive breeding of the Japanese crested ibis, *Nipponia nippon*.' *J. Yamashina Inst. Ornithol.*, vol. 22, no. 1, pp. 70–6.

Ogasawara, K. (1985) 'Acoustic sounds of Japanese crested ibis, *Nipponia nippon*, in Japan and China.' *J. Yamashina Inst. Ornithol.*, vol. 17, no. 2, pp. 127–34.

Shi, D., Yu, X. & Chang, X. (1987) 'The breeding habits of the Japanese crested ibis, *Nipponia nippon*.' Paper presented at the International Conference on Wildlife Conservation in China, Beijing, July 1987. Mimeograph.

Yasuda, K. (1984) 'On a description about colour change on plumage of Japanese crested ibis, *Nipponia nippon*, observed by M. Berezovsky 1884–85.' *J. Yamashina Inst. Ornithol.*, vol. 16, no. 2–3, pp. 174–7.

Golden monkey

Chen, F., Min, Z., Luo, S. & Xie, W. (1983) 'An observation on the behaviour and some ecological habits of the golden monkey, *Rhinopithecus roxellanae*: in Qing Mountains, China.' *Acta Theriol. Sin.*, vol. 3, no. 2, pp. 141–6.

Chen, N. (1992) 'The man who protects Sichuan's golden monkeys.' *China Today*, Feb., pp. 51–2.

Clarke, A.S. (1991) 'Sociosexual behaviour of captive Sichuan golden monkeys, *Rhinopithecus roxellanae*.' *Zoo Biol.*, vol. 10, no. 4, pp. 369–74.

Happel, R. & Cheek, T. (1986) 'Evolutionary biology and ecology of *Rhinopithecus*.' In: Taub, D.M. & King, F.A. (eds) *Current Perspectives in Primate Social Dynamics*. IXth Congress of the International Primatological Society, Atlanta, August 8–13, 1982. Van Nostrand Reinhold, UK and USA.

Laidler, E, (1984) *The Behavioural Ecology of the Giant Otter, Pteronura brasiliensis, in Guyana*. Ph.D. thesis, University of Cambridge.

Li, Z.X., Ma, S.L., Hua, C.H. & Wang, Y.X. (1981) 'The distribution and habits of the Yunnan snub-nosed monkey.' *Dongwuxue Yanjiu*, vol. 2, pp. 9–16.

Ma, S.D. & Wang, Y. (1988) 'The recent distribution, status and conservation of primates in China.' *Acta Theriol. Sin.*, vol. 4, pp. 250–60.

Ma, S., Wang, Y., Jiang, X., Li, J. & Xian, R. (1989) 'Study on the social behaviour and habitual speciality of Yunnan golden monkey.' *Acta Theriol. Sin.*, vol. 9, no. 3, pp. 161–7.

Poirier, F.E. & Hu, H. (1983) '*Macaca mulatta* and *Rhinopithecus* in China; preliminary research results.' *Current Anthropol.*, vol. 24.

Qi, J. (1988) 'Observation studies on reproduction of golden monkey in captivity. I. Copulatory behaviour.' *Acta Theriol. Sin.*, vol. 8, no. 3, pp. 172–5.

Rapaport, L. & Mellen, J.D. (1990) 'Parental care and infant development in a family group of captive Sichuan golden monkeys, *Rhinopithecus roxellanae*: first 20 days.' *Primates* (Japan), vol. 31, no. 1, pp. 129–36.

Shen., P. & Yin, L. (1991) 'Availability of primate species research and management in China.' *J. Primatol.*, vol. 20, no. 8, pp. 382–5.

Shi, D., Li, G. & Hu, T. (1982) 'Primate status and conservation in China.' In: *Primates: the Road to Self-sustaining Populations*. Conference, San Diego, California, June 24–28, 1985. pp. 213–20. Springer-Verlag, USA and Berlin, Germany.

TROPICAL FORESTS

MacKinnon, J., Collins, M. & Green. M. (1991) 'China and Taiwan.' In: Collins, M., Sayer, J.A. & Whitmore, T.C. (eds), *The Conservation Atlas of Tropical Forests*. Macmillan, UK, and Simon & Schuster, USA.

Elephant

Sukumar, R. (1990) 'Ecology of the Asian elephant in southern India. II. Feeding habits and crop-raiding patterns.' *J. Trop. Ecol.*, vol. 6, no. 1, pp. 33–53.

Tang, X. (1987) 'In pursuit of the wild elephant in Xishuangbanna.' In: Tang, X. *Living Treasures. An Odyssey through China's Extraordinary Nature Reserves*. pp. 57–70. Bantam Books Inc. and New World Press.

Gibbons

Ellefson, J.O. (1974) 'A natural history of gibbons in the Malay Peninsula.' In: Rumbaugh, D. (ed.) *Gibbon and Siamang*. Vol. 3, pp. 1–36. S. Karger, Basel.

Ma, S. & Wang, Y. (1988) 'The recent distribution status and conservation of primates in China.' *Acta Theriol. Sin.*, vol. 4, pp. 250–60.

Sung, W. & Guoqiang, Q. (1986) 'Primate status and conservation in China.' In: *Primates: the Road to Self-sustaining Populations*. Conference, San Diego, California, USA, June 24–28, 1985. Springer Verlag, USA and Berlin, Germany.

PICTURE ACKNOWLEDGEMENTS

Ardea 81 (Eric Dragesgo)

Heather Angel 11

Planet Earth Pictures 24–5 (Yuri Shibnev)

Still Pictures 173, 175, 176–7 (Alain Compost), 166–7 (Mark Edwards), 70 (Michael Gunther), 73 (Daniel Heuclin), 181 (Bruno Naso), 54, 60–1, 68–9, 84–5, 153, 179 (Roland Seitre), 157 (J.P. Sylvestre), 124–5, 161, 163 (Pu Tao), 66 (Claude Thouvenin)

Wolfshead 2–3, 7, 13, 19, 26, 30, 31, 33, 36, 39, 51, 78, 88–9, 92, 94, 96–7, 99 (left *and* right), 101, 104, 107, 114, 116–17, 118, 120, 121, 122, 127, 128, 130, 131, 132, 137, 138, 143, 144, 146–7, 148, 155, 168, 184 (Keith and Liz Laidler); 10, 12, 21, 22, 42–3, 44, 46–7, 56–7, 62, 65, 74–5, 90, 110–11, 112, 119, 123, 140, 141, 145, 149, 171 (Ben Osborne).

INDEX